The King's Trouble Makers:

Edenton's Role in Creating a Nation and State

The King's Trouble Makers:

Edenton's Role in Creating a Nation and State

Troy Kickler, Ph.D.

Edenton Historical Commission
Edenton, North Carolina

Published by **Edenton Historical Commission**
(252) 482-7800,
505 South Broad Street,
Edenton, NC 27932,
info@ehcnc.org.

ISBN 978-0-9893275-1-0

Library of Congress control number: 2013955689

Book design by Ray Rhamey

Acknowledgements

Dedicated to all of the Volunteers
who have been sharing these facts
and stories with visitors for decades.

In appreciation of the Edenton Historical Commission members for authorizing this book: C. Christopher Bean, Norman Brinkley, Jr., Jerome F. Climer, Miles B. Coxe, Susan Creighton, William T. Culpepper III, Samuel B. Dixon, John Dowd, A. L. Honeycutt, Jr., Frances Inglis, Don Jordan, SallyFrancis Kehayes, Vann Lassiter, Donna McLees, Thomas Newbern, Frank Palm, Ann Perry, Gail Perry, Elizabeth Pope, Robert Quinn, Simon Rich, Jr., Al Robb, James Robison, Benjamin Speller, Jr., Gary Stanley, Earl Willis, Nancy Winslow, Annette Wood, T. Benbury H. Wood, Jr., Susan Wood and ex-officio members Secretary Susan Kluttz (N.C. Dept. of Cultural Resources), Mayor Roland H. Vaughan (Town of Edenton) and Chairman D. Keith Nixon (Chowan County Board of Commissioners).

In gratitude for the financial support of the Town of Edenton in publishing this work as part of the celebration of the 300th Anniversary of its Founding: Mayor Roland H. Vaughan, Mayor Pro-Tem Jimmy E. Stallings, Councilman Steven W. Biggs, Councilman Samuel B. Dixon, Councilman Willis M. Privott, Councilman Robert Quinn and Councilwoman Norma Jean Simpson.

With special thanks to The King's Trouble Makers committee whose dedication to the project made it a reality: Robert Quinn, Jerome F. Climer, Troy Kickler, Gregg Nathan and Ray Rhamey.

Illustrations

Contents

Preface

If you don't know about Edenton, North Caro-
lina, your knowledge of U.S. history is incomplete
and your knowledge of North Carolina insufficient.
Organized women's political activity in America
was born in Edenton. The concept of judicial review—that courts can declare legislative acts unconstitutional—was first championed here. Ideas for a
national navy and defense were implemented here.
Many passages of the N.C. Constitution (1776) and
the U.S. Constitution originated here. Leading proponents of the U.S. Constitution (a.k.a. Federalists)
lived in this small place, and so did nationally known
jurists and politicians.

Visitors, residents and scholars alike find Edenton and Chowan County interesting places. Some
are intrigued by the 300-year-old collection of architectural gems beginning with the oldest house in
North Carolina, a 1718 colonial cabin still standing
in Edenton.

Other are intrigued by the circumstances that
brought numerous educated and courageous thinkers
to reside in Edenton where they became leaders instructing their representatives to call for independence
from Britain before any other colony. Other leaders
included the woman who showed more courage in

telling a King "NO" than was to be found anywhere else in the emerging country. Another leader, who walked the streets of Edenton on those same days, was so impressive as an articulate, intellectual leader that he was called to sit on the first U.S. Supreme Court.

Still others visitors and residents are captured by the natural beauty of Chowan County from the beautiful creek, Queen Anne's Creek, that gave the first town its name to historic millponds and rivers that accumulate the fresh waters of the great dismal swamp, that stretches miles into Virginia, and send it on to the Atlantic Ocean.

The Edenton Historical Commission has long known these secrets of Edenton and Chowan County and worked to preserve those architectural assets as well as the stories of those leaders who had the courage to become troublemakers for King George and go on to build a nation and a state.

The Commission's experience in operating one of the best North Carolina-focused bookstore and gift shops helped it realize that a major gap existed in telling the story of the birth of our nation and state. There are books about specific leaders but the reader has to work a great deal to develop an understanding how these desperate souls happened to gather at a small town on the banks of the Albemarle Sound, develop working relationships, and ultimately evolve from staunch supporters of the Crown into its harshest critics. These American Patriots then went on to help design and implement the creation of the United States.

The Commission sought a special talent to take that information and blend it into a coherent story about the leadership Edentonians gave to criticizing the Crown and ultimately to demanding independence and forming a new government.

Dr. Troy Kickler recognized from his position as Director of the North Carolina History Project that Edenton was special. In 2010, he established a part-time branch office at Edenton, with the cooperation of the Commission, and spent time here digging deeper into the stories of the leaders from Chowan County.

Troy L. Kickler is Founding Director of the North Carolina History Project and Editor of NorthCarolinahistory.org. He earned his Ph.D. in history from the University of Tennessee. He has written articles and commentaries for various academic and popular publications, including a monthly column for *Carolina Journal,* and he has presented at numerous public venues and academic conferences, including the American Political Science Association.

He has taught at Barton College and North Carolina State University.

He serves on the Scholarly Advisory Board of The Religion in North Carolina Digital Collection, a collaborative project of Duke University, UNC-Chapel Hill, and Wake Forest University. He also serves on the College Level Advisory Board of *Constituting America*, an online essay series exploring the U.S. Constitution, *The Federalist Papers*, and the Founding Era.

Kickler has served on the Board of Trustees for the North Carolina Natural Heritage Trust Fund, and he now currently serves on the Board of Friends of the Archives, a group that provides support for the State Archives of North Carolina.

This book not only tells the story of the leadership that sprang from Edenton and Chowan County, but it also offers two exceedingly important reference tools: a timeline of the country's historic development from 1492 to 1799 and a roster of the important North Carolina characters essential to defining the country and state. The timeline begins on page 77 and the roster of leaders on page 85. Flipping back to check points of reference and or the thumbnail sketches of the leaders can be useful as you read: *The King's Trouble Makers: Edenton's Role in Creating a Nation and State.*

Jerome F. Climer,
Chairman
Edenton Historical Commission
Edenton, NC
2013–300th Anniversary of Edenton's establishment

Introduction

The history in your hand pertains to the Founding Era—a period lasting from approximately 1770 to 1790, a time when the foundations of the United States and North Carolina's polity were laid. In particular, it introduces readers to an important yet often overlooked group of founders of the United States of America. At one time or another, these brave men and women called Edenton, North Carolina or Chowan County, North Carolina home. A small town and county by today's standards, Edenton and Chowan County played an important role not only at the state level but also on the evolving national scene during the Founding Era. In this small place, big ideas were discussed and promoted, and bold action took place.

Edenton was also named one of "America's Prettiest Towns" – Forbes.com, April 12, 2011.

Before I proceed with the introductory narrative of the intellectual and political scene in Edenton and Chowan County, I will take the liberty to relay some pertinent, personal history. When I first visited Edenton, North Carolina, I was struck with the historic district's architectural integrity and understood why the town is known as "The South's Prettiest Small Town." When the traveler steps out of the vehicle, he or she observes that history envelops one, and for some reason the traveler feels compelled to walk around and explore and imagine life and events during the Colonial and Revolutionary periods. At least I did. Whether one realizes it or not, at any given point, significant history is only around the corner, and to be honest, depending on the street you may be walking on, such history may be before the next intersection and the decision to turn left or right. A stroll through town passing historic homes and the historic 1767 Chowan County courthouse, a tour at the Barker House or the Cupola House, a moment to reflect by the waters of the Albemarle Sound, or a time to contemplate at historic St. Paul's Church—all and more opportunities are possible in only a day visit to this quaint town. For full disclosure for the reader, I so enjoyed my visits to Edenton that I now have a satellite office in the town.

As I did more research for various scholarly pursuits, and thereby purposefully and even unintentionally learned more about the town, I concluded that the area is more than architectural gems sitting near the Albemarle Sound. I knew it had been an important place in North Carolina's past, but I did not, at that point, understand to what extent the Town of Edenton and Chowan County contributed to the state's and nation's founding. Edenton and Chowan County comprised a political hub and an intellectual capital of the early United States.

Did you know that Inglis Fletcher's "Carolina Series," about the history of Edenton and North Carolina consisted of 12 novels that were national best sellers?

In 1776, the year the United States of America was born, approximately 600 people lived in the bustling port town of Edenton (by 1786, some "reckoned" 1,000-1,500 souls occupied the town). Among them, some had national importance. During the Founding Era, the town formerly known as Queen Anne's Town, or the Town on Queen Anne's Creek (also known as Matchacamack Creek), was a place that encouraged, supported, and played a definite role in fostering a spirit of independence not only among North Carolinians but also among Americans. Women like Penelope Barker and men like Hugh Williamson, James Iredell, Sr., Samuel Johnston, and Joseph Hewes were known outside their borough and beyond the borders of North Carolina. Stories of their importance will be told in this history's subsequent pages. [1]

Edenton and Chowan County were places in which political protests occurred. The following pages will introduce readers to important and controversial locals, among others, such as Daniel Earl and Penelope Barker. These residents planned political protests against what they deemed an encroachment on American liberties.

Edenton was a town in which intellectuals also discussed ideas—ideas that influenced a broader polity and later judicial decisions, too.

Several delegates to the various Provincial Congresses (North Carolina) and Continental Congresses (United States) called the borough home, too. These representatives made decisions ranging from whether the colony of North Carolina should declare independence from Great Britain to the military preparations during the Revolutionary War.[2]

Many of these same founders later played a significant role in the formation of the United States of America under the U.S. Constitution. They especially played a role at the Constitutional Convention in Philadelphia (1787) and in the 1788 and 1789 North Carolina ratification conventions held, respectively, in Hillsborough and in Fayetteville. In the ratification debates, Edentonians, in particular, played a key role in the intellectual debate. At that time, most

North Carolina was the only colony to hold two U.S. Constitution ratification conventions. (You'll learn why on page 54.)

Edentonians were Federalists, and James Iredell, Sr., was their spokesman. The young Revolutionary pamphleteer turned out to be North Carolina's leading proponent of the U.S. Constitution and later a future U.S. Supreme Court justice. In the contentious debates from 1788 to 1789, he and other Edentonians played an integral part in convincing their fellow North Carolinians to ratify (approve) the U.S. Constitution.[3]

Edenton's influence lasted beyond the Founding Era years. James Iredell later served as a U.S. Supreme Court justice. His opinions on the bench, whether assenting or dissenting, influenced a later constitutional amendment and future judicial decisions. Another legal theorist and U.S. Supreme Court Justice, James Wilson, called Edenton home in his later years. In fact, he was buried on Edentonian Samuel Johnston's property before his body was exhumed and removed and then reinterred and memorialized at Christ Church in Philadelphia, Pennsylvania.

Do you have anything containing the Latin phrase: Novus Ordo Seclorum?

Hint: check your paper money.

The following pages are an introduction to the Town of Edenton and its and Chowan County's role in the formation of the United States, the ratification of the Constitution, and early American constitutional thought. It is a publication to tell others that the foundation of the nation was not laid entirely in Boston, Massachusetts or in Philadelphia, Pennsylvania. Elsewhere, including Edenton and Chowan County, Americans shouldered the burden of laying the foundation, and when the historical record is consulted, one realizes that the small town by Queen Anne's Creek, in many ways, helped shape the formation of the *Novus Ordo Seclorum* (New Order of the Ages) that is called the United States of America.[4]

The Barker House
circa 1782

Chapter One

Edenton Town History

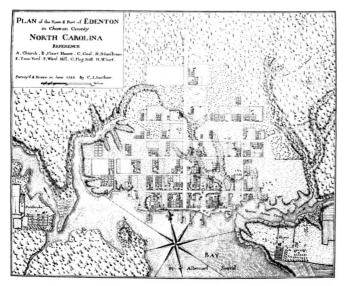

C.J. Sauthier 1769

The following paragraphs explain Edenton's and Chowan County's significant roles in the early days of North Carolina and help readers understand why this area later played such an important role during the Founding Era.

During the late-1600s, the Albemarle region (more or less modern-day northeastern North Carolina) was a safe haven for persecuted Baptists and Quakers. Many of these Protestants originally fled

1

Europe and soon called Virginia home. But many Virginians, members of the Church of England, did not tolerate their low-church brethren. So the Protestant dissidents looked elsewhere for a home. Although the first Europeans migrated to the Albemarle region in the 1650s, more arrived in the late-1600s and early-1700s in a place Virginians later condescendingly called Rogue's Harbor: the Albemarle frontier offered economic opportunity for the religious dissidents, and it was a place in which they could worship freely.[5]

Nathaniel Batts settled in the western part of Albemarle in 1657 and became the first colonist to record a land deed in N.C.

Economic opportunity, however, drew most newcomers to the Albemarle region: land was cheaper than in Virginia, and Edenton, also known as the "Port of Roanoke," was evolving into a bustling port. Many colonists, first and second generations, from Virginia, South Carolina, Pennsylvania, New Jersey, and Maryland embarked on an entrepreneurial adventure that brought them to Edenton. Among Europeans, mainly English settled in the Albemarle region, but there was a sprinkling of Scots and a dash of Irish. During the mid-1700s to late-1700s, more and more Europeans arrived in North Carolina, but they started bypassing the Albemarle to settle mainly in the Cape Fear and Piedmont regions to be mercantile or farming pioneers. Among them, the English, Scots-Irish, Highland Scots, Welsh, Irish, and Germans voluntarily sailed the Atlantic or traveled southward from Northern colonies to North Carolina either for economic opportunity or for a religious or political haven. Meanwhile, newcomers still remained attracted to the Albemarle region and Edenton.[6]

The town's history begins in the early-1700s. A 1712 Act of Assembly encouraged the establishment of a town, then known as the Towne on Queen Anne's Creek. In 1722 it was incorporated and re-named Edenton in honor of Governor Charles Eden, an ironic figure.

Governor Eden gravestone

He not only brought more order to a somewhat lawless Albemarle region but also was allegedly shel-tering Edward Teach, also known as Blackbeard, and promoting piracy and Blackbeard's swashbuckling shenanigans.[7]

Governor Eden allegedly sheltered the pirate Blackbeard, Edward Teach.

Although North Carolina's boundaries extended as far westward into what is now modern-day Ten-nessee, the Albemarle region was synonymous with North Carolina during the state's early years. Eden-ton was the political and economic hub, for the vast majority of North Carolina's political and econom-ic activity occurred in and around the Albemarle Sound.

In 1730, approximately 30,000 whites and 6,000 blacks lived in North Carolina. According to histo-rian Milton Ready, forty-percent of those numbers lived in Chowan County. Another forty-percent lived in the entire Albemarle region that included the following counties: Pasquotank, Perquimans, Tyrell, and Currituck.[8]

The building of a courthouse had made Edenton the seat of government, and the town served exclusively as the colony's capital from 1722-1746. The town was home not only to the courthouse but also to the jail. As a result, many traveled to Edenton to take care of legal transactions, and General Assembly delegates convened there to make decisions for the entire colony.[9]

The town's and region's dominant political influence lasted until the late-1700s. According to historian Robert L. Ganyard, the Albemarle region "enjoyed much stronger representation than did other counties of the colony—so much so that that region dominated the lower house until the middle of the century and exercised an inordinate influence over its proceedings during the remaining of the colonial period."

Indeed in the mid-to-late 1700s, many North Carolinians complained that the region had too much influence in the colonial assembly. Many in the Cape Fear area, in particular, protested in what has been called the "representation controversy." After their town stopped being the colony's capital, Edentonians still played a significant role in North Carolina politics; the town's initial importance had allowed residents to accumulate and invest political and networking capital that reaped rewards in later years.[10]

Francis Corbin served as Lord Granville's proprietary agent from 1744 to 1759, and he was given power of attorney to perform Lord Granville's business in North Carolina. (Lord Granville was the only Lords Proprietor who did not resell land back to the British Crown.) To perform his duties, Corbin opened a land grant office in his house, the Cupola House, in Edenton.

Built in Edenton in 1758 and still standing, the Cupola House was Corbin's land grant office.

Aspiring property holders routinely traveled to town to talk with Corbin. Bishop August Gottlieb Spangenburg, for one, traveled to Edenton to talk with Corbin about purchasing land for a Moravian settlement in the Piedmont. The tract became known as Wachovia.[11]

North Carolina grew exponentially from 1740 to the time of the Revolutionary War in 1776. According to eminent North Carolina historian William S. Powell, the state's population grew from 36,000 in 1730 to almost 265,000 in 1775. Many African slaves were transported to North Carolina, too, and the black population grew exponentially as well: 6,000 in 1730 to approximately 39,000 in 1767, the date of the construction of the 1767 historic Chowan County Courthouse, and then later to 100,000 in 1790.[12]

North Carolina's population grew from 36,000 in 1730 to almost 265,000 in 1775.

Although political power started to shift from the Albemarle region to the Cape Fear region, Edenton and Chowan County remained a mercantile center that attracted the enterprising. Tobacco planters shipped their crops to Edenton to be stored in warehouses and later shipped to other colonies and to Europe. Fisheries dotted the Edenton and Chowan County landscape. It was during this time that James Iredell left England for Edenton, and Joseph Hewes, who originally left New Jersey for Pennsylvania, decided later that Edenton offered economic opportunity. A rector of St. Paul's Church, Daniel Earl, left Ireland and called Chowan County home at his plantation named Bandon. He was an enterprising fellow, and earned a reputation for catching herring in the Albemarle Sound and for improving methods of weaving and preparing flax for the loom. Earl also took advantage of his location near the bountiful Albemarle Sound and earned wealth through his various shad and herring fisheries. (A common fishing method was seine fishing—a net would be dropped into the water and eventually the ends would be drawn up and an abundance of fish would be caught in the net.)[13]

Edenton was a leading port town.

Many goods passed through the port town. From 1771 to 1776, records reveal that 827 ships embarked from Edenton. Approximately one-half were headed for the West Indies. In those five years, locals exported 320,000 bushels of corn and 100,000 barrels of tar on those boats. Daniel Earl no doubt cashed in as 24,000 barrels of fish were exported. According to historian Thomas Parramore, some imports during those five years were the following: rum (250,000 gallons), molasses (100,000 gallons), sugar (600,000 pounds), salt (150,000 pounds), and linen (400,000 yards).[14]

Edenton was a thriving town during the mid-to-late-1700s, as also evidenced by its division and specialization of labor that provided the town's infrastructure. For instance, the town had blacksmiths, lawyers, clergy, craftsmen of various sorts, cabinet-makers, bricklayers, innkeepers, and repairmen. Merchants abounded in the town, and it had more than a few warehouses to store imported goods. According to a Scottish visitor in 1786: "The people are almost all merchants here. They reckon about 1,000 to 1,500 inhabitants in Edenton . . . .The houses are mostly indifferent and built of wood . . . They have a tolerably good brick statehouse, a brick church, and a market place . . . They have a noble ropewalk here, built before the war. . . ." The observer noticed an impressive ropewalk operation east of Edenton. (For more on ropewalking see endnote 15.) It was more than likely Josiah Collins, Sr.'s operation, one of the largest and most profitable in the nation. Sailors needed ropes and cords for their sails and for other shipping functions, and fishermen needed nets to bring in their daily catch. Beginning in 1783, Collins's rope manufacturing business supplied shippers and fishermen with the necessary cords, ropes, and nets to enable them to make a living. The ropewalk remained in operation, under the management of the

Edenton's population was between 1,000 and 1,500 in 1786.

family until 1839.[15]

Edenton attracted many different people, and the various English dialects and accents in the town's streets and market places indicated that diverse people considered the town as a place of opportunity. One could hear Irish, English, and Scottish accents at the market. And no doubt French was heard as well, for Stephen Cabarrus, an Edentonian of French descent and later an influential politician, resided in the town. A disparate people were attracted to a particular place for economic opportunity, and their similar desires united them during the American Revolution and Founding Era.

A disparate people were attracted to Edenton for economic opportunity.

Chapter Two

SEEDS OF INDEPENDENCE

What prompted American colonists, who were proud to be English citizens, to utter phrases, such as Patrick Henry did at St. John's Episcopal Church in Richmond, Virginia on March 23, 1775, "Give me Liberty or give me Death!"? Americans had been loyal subjects to the British Crown and abided by British constitutional and common law. Even when Americans had disagreements with the British Parliament and Crown, an olive branch was figuratively extended, several times, across the Atlantic. What changed American public opinion?

Discontent in the American colonies and in North Carolina began in earnest after the passage of the Sugar Act (1764) and the Stamp Act (1765). The colonies had recently been through the Seven Years War (1756-1763), known to Americans as the French and Indian War. The mother country, England, wanted Americans to pay for a substantial part of their defense in that war and any possible future conflicts. It had cost money to send English troops to the colonies, and it took money to administer a growing empire. The legislation seemed more than reasonable to many British Parliamentarians; the

Political discontent in North Carolina began after passage of the Sugar Act (1764) and the Stamp Act (1765).

American colonies had growing and in some cases thriving economies. Why should the Americans, British Parliamentarians contended, pay less than their fair share? Many British parliamentarians, to be sure, also desired closer supervision and tighter control of the colonies. American colonists, including many North Carolinians, did not appreciate, to put it kindly, what they considered to be English meddling in American affairs. They had been use to legislating their own affairs, and denounced the unprecedented British intrusion.[16]

The Stamp Act particularly angered the colonists, for it touched almost all aspects of commercial and business life. The law required all legal instruments—deeds and bonds, for examples--to be on stamped paper that was printed in England. Without the proper paper, the legal document was not binding. This Parliamentary act also included many exactions: A graduate was taxed for a college diploma, a farmer was taxed for buying an almanac, a businessman was taxed for placing an advertisement in a newspaper, and a couple was taxed for a marriage license. Everywhere a North Carolinian turned, it seemed, in the marketplace or at the courthouse, he was confronted with the Stamp Act.[17]

In 1766 the Stamp Act was repealed.

Sons of Liberty formed to protest the tax. Although the group originated in Boston, Massachusetts, Sons of Liberty groups were formed up and down the Atlantic seaboard after the Stamp Act's passage. In North Carolina, Sons of Liberty sentiment was strongest in the port city of Wilmington, but protests occurred in other towns, including Edenton. Edenton merchants and traders no doubt were thinking like their counterparts in other Northern and Southern port towns, for the interfering legislation affected commercial enterprises.[18]

American protests proved to be effective. In 1766, the Stamp Act was repealed, and British Parliament suffered a crushing blow. Some have argued that this political defeat set the stage for the American Revolution. Why? Royal authority had been weakened, and thereby Americans had been encouraged that their demands could be met. It set a precedent for future models of protest.[19]

For the next ten years, an unsteady relationship existed between Great Britain and her American colonies as contested political interpretations abounded. Parliament still found ways to intervene in the American economy and in American lives. The Townshend Acts, for instance, were passed in 1767 and established a tax on colonial imports of specific British goods. Americans reacted by boycotting British goods. Another example is the passage of the 1773 Tea Act. Americans protested that legislation with protest assemblies and another boycott. The Coercive Acts (known to Americans as "The Intolerable Acts") were passed in 1774; they were a punitive effort to hurt Boston's economy. If it could happen in Boston, Americans speculated, it could happen anywhere in the American colonies. So Americans called for a Continental Congress, and each respective colony elected delegates to discuss an American response to British Parliamentary encroachment.[20]

In the early 1770s, though, Edenton and Chowan County seemed unlikely to take up arms against Great Britain. In fact, many Edentonians, especially Samuel Johnston, had sided with the Royal Governor, and in essence the Crown of England during the Regulator Rebellion (1768-1771)--a protest by Piedmont farmers against what the agrarians deemed

For the next ten years, an unsteady relationship existed between Great Britain and her American colonies.

In the early- 1770s, though, Edenton and Chowan County seemed unlikely to take up arms against Great Britain.

excessive legal fees and corruption in local governments. According to historian William S. Powell, the Regulator Movement was a "struggle for political rights and individual liberty denied by provincial and local governments."[21]

Much happened, however, between 1771 and 1775, and there was indeed a budding spirit of independence growing in the hearts of Americans. Although North Carolina had a significant number of Loyalists, the regional tensions within the state seemed to lighten. At least James Iredell, Sr., thought so. "Regulation is a name scarcely remembered, and all busy Spirits are at peace," he wrote. As a delegate to the Fourth Provincial Congress meeting in Halifax, he voted with other delegates unanimously (81-0) for the passage of the Halifax Resolves. It was a convincing expression of general opinion, as Samuel Johnston notably stated a few days before its passage in 1776: "All our people here are up for Independence."[22]

Samuel Johnston said: "All our people here are up for Independence."

REVOLUTIONARY ERA "NEWS JUNKIES"

Edentonians were politically aware and up-to-date regarding the latest political developments and were knowledgeable concerning how the past can influence the present.

This is evidenced by James Iredell's diary entries. On one day after rising from bed, Iredell read legal theorist William Blackstone's scholarship until breakfast. Later in the morning, he conversed with his wife, Hannah, who was the sister of an influential politician, Samuel Johnston. After conversing with Hannah, he visited with some town notables and with Cornelius Harnett and wife. Harnett was a leading Patriot from the Wilmington area and had been

Hannah, Samuel Johnston's sister, was James Iredell's wife.

a leading opponent of the Stamp Act (1765); the couple arrived to visit specifically with Joseph Hewes, a future signatory of the Declaration of Independence. James Iredell, for whatever reason, decided to pay a visit. Considering those sitting within the walls of Hewes's home, discussions no doubt took a political turn.[23]

On another day, Iredell read a good portion of a biography of the Earl of Shaftesbury, Anthony Ashley Cooper. He was one of the eight Lords Proprietors of Carolina, and a patron of John Locke, the political philosopher, who was also the Earl's doctor. (The two rivers in Charleston, the Ashley and the Cooper, were named for the Earl of Shaftesbury.) Historians have concurred that John Locke played an instrumental role in writing the Fundamental Constitutions of Carolina (1669). It is the charter and earlier constitutions that Edentonians, such as James Iredell and Hugh Williamson, later referred to when making arguments that the British Parliament overstepped its authoritative boundaries and encroached on guaranteed liberties. Also in the diary, Iredell notes that he later talked with Samuel Johnston, his brother-in-law who referred to himself in letters as Iredell's "brother."[24]

Did you know that John Locke played an instrumental role in writing the Fundamental Constitutions of Carolina (1669)?

In personal correspondence, Edentonians discussed current events and revealed a sophisticated knowledge of history. Edenton's James Iredell and Wilmington's William Hooper, an influential North Carolina politician and later a signer of the Declaration of Independence, relayed information regarding current events to each other and opined regularly from 1773 onward. Joseph Hewes's correspondence, to name another example, kept James Iredell informed as to what occurred at the Continental Congress. (After

In 1773 the Boston Tea Party occurred.

the violence in Boston in 1773, North Carolina Whigs, including Joseph Hewes of Edenton, started creating extralegal assemblies to discuss and make plans to thwart what colonists considered unconstitutional actions.) In April 1774, Iredell opened and read another correspondence from Hooper: "They [North Carolinians and all American colonists] are striding fast to independence, and ere long will build an empire upon the ruin of Great Britain." Three weeks prior, Chowan countian Samuel Johnston corresponded with Hooper concerning a conversation he had with Colonel John Harvey of Perquimans County. The colonel was most displeased with Royal Governor Josiah Martin and wanted to "issue handbills under his own name," Johnston went on, and called for a committee of correspondence to "go to work at once." Johnston was at a loss of ideas as to what must be done to assuage an "alarmed and dissatisfied" community. But something, he argued to Hooper, must be attempted.[25]

A WIRE SERVICE
BEFORE THERE WAS A WIRE SERVICE

Literate Edentonians were, to use a modern description, "news junkies." The insatiable appetite to consume news motivated at least 27 Edentonians, including Samuel Johnston, James Iredell, and a few members of St. Paul's Vestry, to contract with Robert Smith to hire a rider to bring "the earliest news and Intelligence" from Suffolk, Virginia, during what town residents described as "Present Critical times."

The date was May 6, 1775, a year in which political protests increased, the debates against Parliamentary encroachment intensified, and the American colonies moved methodically toward independence.

It would not have been uncommon to see town residents carrying or sharing newspapers or broadsides from other American colonies, and even from abroad.[26]

Suffolk subscription list

Being up-to-date fueled their robust conversations.

No doubt, hallways in Edenton's homes were abuzz with political conversations, and no doubt men and women, both, participated in the discussions; Iredell, for instance, visited leading Revolutionary Cornelius Harnett and his wife in Hewes's home, and in his letters to his wife, Hannah, James Iredell mentioned politics as well as domestic matters. Women were aware of the political hot topics, as evidenced by what is known as the Edenton Tea Party (see subsequent section "Disenchantment and Evolving Whiggery").

Edenton women were aware of political hot topics.

These news pages further informed Edentonians' communications regarding events leading up to the Revolutionary War and ultimately American independence and the formation of a new nation. William Hooper was also a delegate to the 1776 Continental Congress being held in Philadelphia. He once relayed information to Iredell concerning the build-up of a Continental Army and the need for a Navy. And in so doing, he discussed the necessity of virtue in a new nation. He also mentioned news stories from which he learned about the Patriotic spirit evinced in Edenton and Chowan County. Joseph Hewes's duties as Secretary of the Naval Board required him to be well informed. In this capacity, he communicated with the famous John Paul Jones who wrote to the Edentonian on May 19, 1776 regarding proper qualifications for a naval officer.[27]

Edenton's Joseph Hewes was Secretary of the Naval Board.

Edenton and Chowan County were hubs of the American and North Carolinian economy and politics. Not only did townspeople read news in broadsides and discuss current events in their parlors sipping tea, or at the local tavern drinking a pint of beer or sipping rum, the sheer number of shippers from other colonies, going in and out of the port, provided a news source, even if only hearsay, for the curious population.

Chapter Three

DISENCHANTMENT AND EVOLVING WHIGGERY

In 1773, the Boston Tea Party occurred and future Edentonian Hugh Williamson had witnessed it. Many North Carolinians approved the actions of the approximately fifty Bostonians who had dumped tea into the local harbor as a protest to the Tea Act. So other Americans started emulating the Bostonians. Indeed, boycotts and tea parties became a popular form of protest up and down the American coastline in 1773 and 1774. Such a protest occurred in Edenton.[28]

In the American colonies, Whigs supported independence and were also known as Patriots.

Penelope Barker

This protest was different, however. Led by Penelope Barker, women in Edenton and the Chowan County area signed a petition to boycott English goods and protest the tax. Their action was the first organized political activity by women in what became the United States. Although signing a petition seems benign and somewhat routine by modern-day political activism standards, this arena had been previously reserved for men. By simply signing a petition, the "patriotic ladies" performed a bold political action when stepping--intentionally stepping--into the political, public sphere. The women did so, according to the petition, because it was a duty. It was owed, in their words, to their "near and dear connections." Silence or inaction, it seems they believed, equaled irresponsibility as the slightest offense or betrayal as the worst offense to their community. As the women put it, they could not be "indifferent on any occasion that appear[ed] nearly to affect the peace and happiness of our country."[29]

Did you know that in 1774 Benedict Arnold's ship docked at Edenton?

What has become known as the Edenton Tea Party attracted attention across the Atlantic Ocean, for a political first had occurred in the town in October 1774. "The Association Signed by the Ladies of Edenton, North Carolina" appeared later in an English publication, the *Morning Chronicle and London Advertiser.* English cartoonists, not surprisingly, mocked the affair. Many English sardonically questioned what was happening in Edenton. Were men behaving like women? Were women now behaving like men? [30]

James Iredell more or less fielded questions from his brother, Arthur, a London resident, whose interest had been piqued by media accounts describing the provocative leadership of Penelope Barker and

The Edenton Tea Party, 1774

A SOCIETY of PATRIOTIC LADIES,
AT
EDENTON in NORTH CAROLINA.

Plate V.

the Edenton women's pesky behavior. "Pray are you becoming patriotic?," he asked. "Is there a Female Congress at Edenton, too?" Probably disguising genuine concern in the form of humor, a common psychological coping mechanism, Arthur Iredell continued: "If the Ladies, who have ever, since the Amazonian Era, been esteem[e]d the most formidable Enemies, if they, I say, should attack us, the most fatal consequence is to be dreaded. So dexterous in the handling of a dart, each wound they give is mortal . . . The more we try to conquer them, the

Were Edenton women now behaving like men? So wondered James Iredell's brother Arthur.

19

more we are conquered . . . There are but few places in America which possess so much female artillery as Edenton."[31]

The men of Edenton did more than talk or write about being Patriotic. Some members of Edenton's Committee of Safety earned a reputation for occasional zealous expressions of Whiggery, or to be more descriptive and accurate, violence. Committees of Safety were formed in other locales in the state—Fayetteville, New Bern, and Wilmington--and in other American colonies.

A brief note of explanation is in order. In many locations by 1774, Committees of Safety had grown out of the former Sons of Liberty groups. Members were watchdogs on the royal government and monitored any expressions of Tory sentiment in their communities. The Edenton Committee, at times, even questioned conservative Samuel Johnston's patriotism. The notable had befriended Loyalists, and during and after the Revolutionary War, he defended the property rights of Tories. Committees of Safety were in effect parallel governments that evolved and helped form independent American colonies in 1776.[32]

The local Committee of Safety was criticized for its occasional zealotry. Such was deemed the case with Cullen Pollok, a local Scot who had allegedly expressed Loyalist sentiment. Pollok was detained for a night to justify his words and actions to the Edenton committee. When the committee dismissed his case, Pollok no doubt dropped his shoulders as he exhaled a sigh of relief. He may have forgotten, though, that in his defense he disrespected—or so they thought--certain militia officers. The offended wanted retribution. That night, allegedly sodden, a

A teapot on a cannon.

After Cullen Pollok had been tarred and feathered, his tormentors returned to his house and adding insult to injury: they drank his stock of liquor.

few militiamen invaded the Pollok household and dragged the Scot, with a bewildered and screaming wife in pursuit, to be tarred and feathered. Afterward, no doubt an embarrassing moment for Pollok, Committee members returned to his house and "drank his stock of liquor."[33]

Many Patriots, from Edenton and elsewhere, thought the Committee of Safety's reaction--rather a few of its members' behavior that included two vestryman of St. Paul's Church--was zealous, unnecessary, and hurt the Patriot cause. Wilmingtonian William Hooper wrote, "Surely such violence never begat Converts, such violence hurts the cause." Afterward, Chowan County's Samuel Johnston, a Patriot and a Scotland native, provided the Pollok family boarding and protection at his house until cooler heads in town prevailed.[34]

More than likely, militiamen were aware that Royal Governor Josiah Martin had been recruiting Scots, and some ardent Patriots had a tendency to lump all into the Loyalist category. (Indeed Highlanders from the Fayetteville area clashed with Patriots in February 1776, months before the signing of the Declaration of Independence, at the Battle of Moore's Creek.) Some like Robert Smith of Edenton believed Scots were profiled and targeted. "The times here begin to be very troublesome. They Tarr'd & feathered two poor Devils last week and set them Over to Tyrell, this week they threaten to serve all my Country men the same way."[35]

THE TEST

One thing is for sure: Patriot sentiment was intense and prevalent in the Edenton and Chowan County area. Before the Declaration of Independence

The Vestry of St. Paul's approved "The Test" on June 19, 1776—fifteen days before July 4th.

was penned, Edentonians started steering the state and nation toward independence. In August 1774, Daniel Earl, the rector of St. Paul's Church, gathered many townsmen and many of his parishioners outside the courthouse and denounced the Boston Port Act and the British encroachment on liberties in the port town. He read from what was called "Resolutions by the Inhabitants of Chowan County" (see endnote 36 for the document's full title). The document had been approved earlier "at a very respectable and numerous Meeting of the Freeholders of the County of Chowan and Town of Edenton, and other Inhabitants of the said County and Town, at the Court House in Edenton."[36]

Even in "Resolutions by the Inhabitants of Chowan County," Edentonians and Chowan County residents expressed loyalty to King George III, as long as the Crown performed "just and legal exercise of powers vested in him by the British Constitution"; however, they declared Parliamentary actions on "taxes and duties" to be "Arbitrary and unjust." Such creeping encroachment on liberty, they feared, threatened to destroy their "natural rights and privileges" guaranteed by the colonial charter. (As evidenced by James Iredell's later publications, colonial charters in America were referenced many times during political speeches and in revolutionary pamphlets.) The gathered assembly in front of the courthouse wanted all five of their Provincial Congressional delegates to carry out their wishes. On that hot and humid summer day, they instructed their representatives to carry out the "Resolutions" at the Provincial Congress.[37]

Indeed, the spirit of independence was gaining momentum in Chowan County and North Carolina and the American colonies. So much so, that in June 1776, a month before the signing of the Declaration of Independence, the Vestry of St. Paul's Church in Edenton issued a "Test." As Parson Earl had previously done, the Vestry expressed allegiance to the King in the document while condemning Parliamentary action to "impose taxes" on the American colonies. All such encroachments and violations of the British constitution, however, were to be "resisted to the utmost." The Vestry furthermore pledged to "maintain and support" the decisions of the Continental and Provincial Congresses."

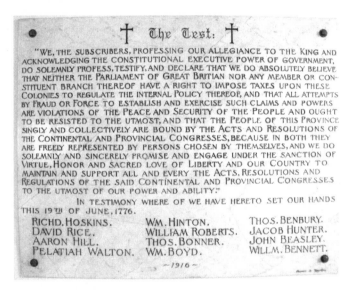

By expressing allegiance to the Crown, the Vestry of St. Paul's offered one more olive branch to Great Britain in hopes of restoring what colonists considered proper and constitutional British rule. Yet its action was bold and revolutionary, and the Test reflected the growing spirit of independence evolving in the American colonies months before the signing of the Declaration of Independence.[38]

The Barker House
circa 1782

Chapter Four

AN INTELLECTUAL CAPITAL
IN DISRUPTIVE TIMES

Edenton was not only a place of action, a hub bustling with what modern-day Americans might call grassroots activity; it was an intellectual capital of North Carolina and the United States. It was a "flourishing" place during the Revolutionary War. More than a few intellectuals hailed from Edenton and Chowan County or later in their life resided in the area. They provided the legal and intellectual ammunition for those Americans who picked up the musket and sword, and in some cases pitchforks, against the British.[39]

James Iredell, Sr.

One such figure was James Iredell, a leading pamphleteer during the Revolutionary War and later a U.S. Supreme Court justice. The young lawyer from Edenton wielded the quill and on parchment penned *To The Inhabitants of Great Britain* (1774) and later *Principles of An American Whig* (1775).

In *To the Inhabitants of Great Britain,* the young legal scholar appeals to the British, a people he describes as being concerned with constitutional principles. To gain their attention and political sympathy, Iredell points out that American colonists, who were English, and the English in the Isle of Britain both consider the British Constitution as the cornerstone of their rule of law. They had much in common: American colonists had the same constitutional rights as the English because they were Englishmen. And North Carolinians, in particular argued Iredell, received the "blessings of the British Constitution" via the Crown's agreement with colonists in the various colonial charters. The rights "bestowed" on American colonists should "never be infringed," at least by the British Parliament. In making this argument, Iredell countered the writings of a leading British legal authority, William Blackstone, who argued that Parliament's sovereignty could not be limited or divided throughout the British Empire. Patriots considered the challenge gutsy; Parliamentarians more than likely deemed it impudence.[40]

Throughout *To the Inhabitants,* to be sure, Iredell hearkens back to the colonial charters that guaranteed liberties among Americans. (As will be recalled, North Carolina's was written in 1663, and the philosopher and mentor of Ashley Cooper, John Locke, played an instrumental role in writing the fundamental rule of law in the Carolina colony). One of

Iredell contended: The rights "bestowed" on American colonists should "never be infringed,. . . ."

Iredell's main concerns, like Locke's, was property rights. He in particular stresses the importance of the House of Commons in North Carolina, for that legislative body, in Iredell's mind, was the sovereign, law-making entity in the colony under the British Constitution. He argued that the Carolina Charter and Fundamental Constitutions had granted Carolina, and later North Carolina and its legislative body, the power to tax and make laws for those living within its borders. In making his case, Iredell denounced the idea of virtual representation—the idea that those elected by voters in England to British Parliament, alone, should be able to make decisions for American colonists. North Carolina was being silenced in a legislative body passing laws affecting North Carolinians. In other words, it was taxation without representation. Either the North Carolina House of Commons should make such decisions independently of Parliament, or North Carolina should have delegates, a voice, in the British Parliament.[41]

Jefferson described the British Parliament's actions as "foreign to our constitutions, and unacknowledged by our laws."

Iredell put forth this argument the same year Thomas Jefferson wrote a similar one in *Summary View of the Rights of British America*. The Virginian and future third President of the United States described the British Parliament as "a body of men" who committed "acts of power. . . foreign to our constitutions, and unacknowledged by our laws." Jefferson believed that there was no central government that legislated for the entire British Empire. Each colony had provincial legislatures in which respective colonists ruled themselves.[42]

In "Principles of an American Whig," Iredell expressed many grievances similar to what was later expressed in the Declaration of Independence.

In *Principles of an American Whig*, Iredell expressed many grievances similar to what was later expressed in the Declaration of Independence. The similarities are not surprising; American founders read each other's writings and corresponded regularly. They were having a conversation, whether face-to-face or in print. To be sure, not all founders knew each other, but at the very least, something was in the air--an American zeitgeist inspiring American legal theorists and political thinkers to address the same concerns.[43]

Although courageous, Iredell was not quite revolutionary in *Principles.* In it, Iredell once again expressed his willingness to abide by Crown rule. What he wanted, and as did the majority of colonists, was for the Crown and Parliament to return to proper and constitutional rule.[44]

More specifically, *Principles* describes nineteen general principles applicable to the American economic and political situation in 1775. The Edenton lawyer writes that God intended for mankind to be happy and that the constitution of Britain is a means for Americans to be happy and enjoy the fruits of their labor. Iredell foresaw an America heading down a path ending at tyranny. The nineteenth and final principle is the following: "That, as in most other countries which have been cursed by the unfeeling rigor of despotism, insidious arts and plausible pretences have been the forerunners of its success, so in America such arts and pretences have been very liberally used." [45]

Iredell describing the attack on Boston: "... for their mutual defence; such an union was absolutely necessary for their safety; singly they might be easily crushed."

Iredell then suggests a different course—a unified American defense. In *Principles,* Iredell identifies with Bostonians, also known as "the people of Massachusetts Bay," and their defense of liberty. He ends this essay by claiming that all American colonists were concerned about the "principle" of Parliamentary legislation. Although he avoids denouncing the Crown, his ending words reflect a definite willingness to consider independence: "Their [Bostonians'] rights were nearly the same; an invasion of one was equivalent to a declaration of war against the rest. Heaven had placed them in the neighborhood of each other, as it were, for their mutual defence; such an union was absolutely necessary for their safety; *singly* they might be easily crushed."[46]

Iredell's arguments were impressive. The influential North Carolinian William Hooper contacted Iredell after reading the young lawyer's work; Samuel Johnston had recommended that Hooper read Iredell's writings. On April 26, 1774, Hooper struck up a conversation—in letters, of course—with the Edentonian: "To your most intimate friends, I am indebted for the discovery of you as a writer." Iredell's writing style was clear and forceful yet remained respectful. As Hooper relayed: "You have discussed dry truths with the most pleasing language; and have not parted from the most refined delicacy of manners in the warmth of the contest." In short, Iredell was persuasive writer.[47]

An appreciative Hooper describing Iredell's writings, said: "... I am indebted for the discovery of you as a writer."

Iredell's pleas to the government of Great Britain, however, fell on deaf ears, and in mid-1776 he soon expressed a definite spirit of independence that mirrored the area's galvanizing political views. Although initially a reluctant Revolutionary, James Iredell revealed passionate opinions--in private, of course--during the time of the signing of the Declaration of Independence in Philadelphia. In a 1776 letter to his good friend Thomas Jones of Edenton, the young lawyer wrote: "O! Britain, miserable unhappy Country! Losing half its dominion, and greatly endangering the other half, by the mismanagement, villainy, and perfidious ambition of a set of Rascals, destined it would appear by fate, to be the horrid instruments of destroying their country." Iredell wished events

Iredell, by mid-1776, reached a tipping-point and intellectually and emotionally joined the revolution.

had turned out differently, but times demanded a different course of action. One could not overlook British Parliamentary encroachment any more.[48]

Chapter Five

EDENTON AND THE YEARS OF INDEPENDENCE

The future U.S. Supreme Court justice was definitely not alone in Edenton. As written previously, the Vestry of St. Paul's Church had, more or less, declared independence from Great Britain. One Edentonian, Joseph Hewes, and two other North Carolinians joined 52 other Patriots and signed the Declaration of Independence.

Joseph Hewes

By doing so, Hewes, with fellow North Carolinians William Hooper of Wilmington and John Penn of Granville County, risked their economic fortunes and professional reputations, as well as their lives. One wonders what the signers thought immediately before placing their signatures on that document for the British Crown and the world to see.

Let me offer here a brief biographical note regarding Joseph Hewes, a successful merchant. He was representative of the mid-eighteenth-century financial success in the American colonies that prompted the British Parliament to pass more tax laws on Americans after the French and Indian War. At 30 years old, Hewes moved from Pennsylvania to Edenton, North Carolina and brought his entrepreneurial savvy with him. Although he knew almost no one on arrival, the merchant soon became popular and earned respect. So much so that six years later he served in the colonial legislature and later as a delegate to a 1774 Continental Congress and on a 1775 Committee of Correspondence. He gained respect in that soon-to-be-national body. At the Continental Congress, Hewes served on one committee that drafted ten declarations of rights to protect the sovereignty of each respective colony. North Carolinians were satisfied with Hewes's performance as a statesman, as argued in an entry on northcarolinahistory.org: "North Carolinians were pleased with Hewes's [prior] representation and reelected him to Congress in 1775." As a delegate to the Second Continental Congress, Edenton's Hewes had the opportunity to sign the Declaration of Independence. [49]

Edenton's Joseph Hewes, a delegate to the Second Continental Congress, signed the Declaration of Independence.

Before the signing of the Declaration of Independence and before July 4, 1776, however, a spirit of independence had existed in North Carolina.

The Halifax Resolves was passed on April 12, 1776. North Carolina's delegates at the Continental Congress, William Hooper and John Penn and Edenton's Joseph Hewes knew that a document such as the Halifax Resolves needed to be passed and were hesitant to proceed until empowered to do so. Without it, North Carolinians might not have accepted any agreements and resolutions or any documents coming down from Philadelphia as authoritative.

After little debate at Halifax, the Fourth Provincial Congress voted (81-0) to empower North Carolina delegates at the Continental Congress to negotiate with delegates from other colonies. As historian Don Higginbotham writes: "The deed was done, and North Carolina was the first colony to permit its contingent in [the Continental] Congress to vote for independence." In the words of Edenton's Samuel Johnston in a note to James Iredell: "The House . . . last night agreed to impower their Delegates at Philadelphia to concur with other Colonies in entering into foreign Alliances and declaring an independence on Great Britain. I cannot be more particular." The Halifax Resolves were later published and distributed to interested parties in other colonies as a "laudable example." [50]

"The deed was done, and North Carolina was the first colony to permit its contingent in [the Continental] Congress to vote for independence."

The Barker House
circa 1782

Chapter Six

STATE CONSTITUTION AND GOVERNMENT

Now what? Many Americans must have asked that question after declaring independence. To decry government encroachment and ultimately separate from Great Britain was indeed a bold move. It was something else entirely to start a new government and to be truly independent.

Provincial Wax Seal, property of Edenton Historical Commission

After the Declaration of Independence, North Carolina needed a state constitution and a new form of government, and the fledgling United States needed a form of government and a constitution, a rule of law. Edentonians played a key role in the formation of each.

Across North Carolina on October 15, 1776, elections in thirty-five counties and in nine towns were held to elect representatives to North Carolina's November congress.

Although there is no historical record pertaining to the electoral process and events in Chowan County, historian Robert L. Ganyard, in his *The Emergence of North Carolina's Revolutionary State Government,* writes that "Tradition has it that a riotous and bitter election. . ." was held and that the "radicals," vigorously ". . . exerted all their efforts to bring about the defeat of Samuel Johnston. . . ." The records are silent whether the "conservative" Johnston even ran for office. It is not far-fetched, considering his status, for him to have desired an official voice regarding the drafting of the new state constitution. We do know that Johnston's name is absent from the list of those serving in the Fifth Provincial Congress. As written previously, Johnston, a native Scot, had befriended some Tories in the area and treated them more benignly than did some of his Patriot counterparts. If he did run for election, those practices, not his political views, more than likely troubled his more Whiggish neighbors in Chowan County. After the election, "conservative" Chowan County residents—Thomas Jones, Thomas Benbury, and James Blount—represented the county in the North Carolina House of Commons. Representing the town of Edenton, Joseph Hewes joined them.[51]

A state constitution and a declaration of rights were to be drafted at the Fifth Provincial Congress. Nothing less than the foundation and structure of the new state government was to be laid and built.

A state constitution and a declaration of rights were to be drafted at the Fifth Provincial Congress.

Out of the assembly, sixteen delegates representing North Carolina's geographical diversity, were chosen to serve on a committee that constructed the state constitution. Edenton's Joseph Hewes and Chowan County's Thomas Jones were among them and represented Albemarle interests. Thomas Jones must have been the chair; he read drafts of the constitution to the entire body for their approval or amendment, and the first state constitution has been referred to as "Jones's constitution."[52]

The first state constitution came to be known as the Jones's Constitution, named for the Chowan County delegate.

The Instructions of Mecklenburg County, the Instructions of Orange County, and William Hooper's letter to the Provincial Congress were attempts to steer the direction of the committee into a more radical or more conservative direction. In addition to considering the political pressure from Mecklenburg and Orange counties and Hooper's widespread influence, members consulted John Adams's "Thoughts on Government" and the various state constitutions that had been previously drafted and approved. They furthermore, as Ganyard states, consulted history, and, "the natural rights, compact theory as expounded by John Locke, with which colonial politicians were so familiar." To put it more clearly, they referred to the colonial charters and the first constitution of Carolina, and the British constitution— a common practice by North Carolina intellectuals during the American Revolutionary period.[53]

Delegates to the Fifth Provincial Congress consulted the writings of John Adams, John Locke, constitutions of other colonies and even the British constitution as they debated the conflicting, but developed philosophies on governance of their own delegates.

To unite a diverse state that went from the Atlantic Ocean to as far west as claims to the Mississippi River, the committee incorporated some "radical" and "democratic" elements and some "conservative" elements. Some historians divide the delegates into three camps—radical, conservative, and more or less, to use a modern description, moderate; other historians have delineated only two—democratic and conservative. On many issues, the divide fell along regional lines. One thing is for sure: differing opinions were espoused in Halifax that year. As historian John W. Moore writes, "It was a clash of political views representing those of Samuel Johnston of Edenton"—even though he was not a part of the official Fifth Provincial Congress (he was aware of it happenings, however)—"and Willie Jones of Halifax County." The former, according to the 1882 history, thought that "new experiments in government were dangerous . . ." and "doubted the ability of people to govern themselves." The latter, who ironically owned a large number of slaves, believed that "the American people were capable of governing themselves, and that all political power belonged to and proceeded from them."[54]

Indeed, Hooper was influential. He had written a letter to the Constitution Committee, with Joseph Hewes and Thomas Jones as members. And it was Hooper, along with John Penn of Granville County, who had asked John Adams for his ideas regarding government. Those two signatories of the Declaration of Independence prompted Adams's "Thoughts on Government," an essay with ideas and language similar to those expressed in Iredell's 1775 *Principles of an American Whig*. Both essayists remarked, in their own words, that government is based on virtue, and the purpose of government is the happiness of people.[55]

After much debate, the delegates approved the North Carolina Constitution of 1776 on December 18, 1776. Representation and districting, voting requirements, and the state and local court systems were issues that were settled, to name three examples.

The constitution limited gubernatorial power and gave the General Assembly the power to elect the governor and the Council of State. The document provided for a bicameral (two-house) legislature: a Senate and a House of Commons.[56]

The Provincial Congress also approved a Declaration of Rights. The twenty-five delineated rights reinforced the idea that government "is the creation of the people" and government answers to them. Individuals, it was believed, possess certain "fundamental, unalienable, and inviolable natural rights" that the government should protect and not encroach upon. The Declaration of Rights later served as a model for the crafting of the future Bill of Rights, the first ten amendments to the U.S. Constitution.[57]

After the state constitution had been approved, the Provincial Congress voted for a governor and Council of State. Richard Caswell was elected the first governor. Some historians have described him as a voice of moderation and a "man of excellent discretion and great political common sense." His peers also considered him to be such a man, a genuine leader, with the ability to influence "men of strong convictions" and persuade them to work together.

The North Carolina Provincial Congress also approved a Declaration of Rights. The twenty-five delineated rights reinforced the idea that government "is the creation of the people" and government answers to them.

Richard Caswell was elected the first Governor under the new North Carolina Constitution.

The Barker House
circa 1782

Chapter Seven

CREATING A NATIONAL GOVERNMENT

Samuel Johnston

Although no Edentonians were on the Council of State, the town's influence was felt on the budding national level. The General Assembly elected the esteemed Joseph Hewes to be a delegate at the Continental Congress. The town's legal scholar, James Iredell, was one of three judges to be appointed on the superior court.[58]

The states eventually agreed to a national form of government under a constitution called the Articles of Confederation. Although the Articles were drafted in the Second Continental Congress in Philadelphia and submitted to the states for ratification in 1777, it did not take effect until 1781 with all thirteen states' approval. Even so, the Continental Congress convened and legislated beforehand in anticipation of the Articles approval. North Carolina approved the Articles on April 24, 1778.

The post-war states agreed to a national form of government under a constitution called the Articles of Confederation.

The Articles ensured that the newly formed states retained much of their sovereignty. At the time, the national government, according to William S. Powell, was unable to "raise money directly, to enlist troops directly, or to regulate commerce." In essence, state governments at that time had more power over citizens within the respective border than did the national government. The United States could not directly tax Americans; only the North Carolina legislature could directly levy taxes on North Carolinians. States were more or less independent entities. But there were things that states could not do. They could not, writes Powell, enter into treaties or "wage war without congressional consent unless invaded"—to name two examples.[59]

Under the Articles of Confederation, the U.S. government could not directly tax Americans; only the North Carolina legislature could directly levy taxes on North Carolinians.

Under the Articles, the national branch had one agency—Congress. In it, each state had a delegation, but no matter the size of the delegation, each state had equal power--one vote. Congressional decisions must be unanimous, for one dissent stopped the passage

The national government had one agency or branch, Congress, under the new Articles of Confederation.

of legislation. The purposeful design ensured that states maintained more power than the national government.

Although Samuel Johnston was not elected, for whatever reason, to the Fifth Provincial Congress, he in no way disappeared from the political scene. Samuel Johnston won a state senate election in 1779, and in 1780 North Carolina's legislature selected him to represent the state at the Continental Congress. The delegates in that national body elected him chairman, a position that would have essentially made him the president of that legislative body and more or less the executive of the United States.[60]

He declined, and his reason remains a mystery. It is possible that Johnston realized that he had more power and influence in America while working within the North Carolina Assembly than he could have holding the top position in the national government. An interesting note is that Johnston served as president of the 1789 North Carolina convention in Fayetteville that ratified the Constitution, and shortly afterward, he accepted when the state legislature elected him to serve as one of North Carolina's first U.S. Senators.

Edenton's Samuel Johnston was elected president of the Congress, in essence the chief executive of the new country. He declined to serve.

THE BIRTHPLACE OF JUDICIAL REVIEW?

After the Revolutionary War ended, Johnston and his brother-in-law James Iredell still practiced law in Edenton and North Carolina. As practicing attorneys, they participated in a first in American judicial history in 1787. The two Edenton lawyers defended a Tory whose property had been seized by the North Carolina legislature. The legal team persuaded a North Carolina court to void the state's confiscation act. Although they lost the case on other grounds,

James Iredell, Sr.

Iredell's arguments in "Bayard v. Singleton" established the precedents followed by Chief Justice Marshall in the famous "Marbury v. Madison" case defining the court's authority to declare Congressional actions unconstitutional.

Bayard v. Singleton, as historian Jeff Broadwater writes, was one of the first examples of judicial review in American history. It set a precedent for the U.S. Supreme Court, under Chief Justice John Marshall in *Marbury v. Madison* (1803), a case in which the Court ruled a congressional act to be unconstitutional.[61]

Edenton's lawyers were known, far and wide. Elizabeth Cornell Bayard, the daughter of Samuel Cornell, hired Samuel Johnston to represent her at the Court of Conference, the state's predecessor of the modern-day North Carolina Supreme Court. Historians believe Spyers Singleton asked Iredell to represent the defense, but Iredell turned down the job. Probably no one who knew the attorney was surprised; he once served as Johnston's legal apprentice, and he was also the brother-in-law of his former boss. Moreover, he had defended publicly the concept of judicial review in a pamphlet titled "To The Public."[62]

Johnston, a Scot, had been a Patriot during the American Revolution, but he had always been sympathetic to the plight of Tories in his ardent Whig region. He had supported the royal governor during the Regulator Rebellion, and he had been slow to champion the Patriot cause. As written previously, he had provided shelter for the Pollok family after a few zealous militiamen tarred and feathered the Scot. His peers considered him a "conservative" which meant in those days that one liked certain aspects of the British government and hoped to incorporate them, such as property qualifications for voters, into the new state and national governments. His patriotism was never seriously questioned, but his legal and political peers were probably not surprised when he represented a former Tory in 1787.[63]

The overall historical context of the case was as follows. The state passed confiscation acts in 1777 and 1779. In them, the state declared that Loyalists' property could be seized and sold. Why? The state needed money to pay for the war effort during the American Revolution. The state took, as J. Edwin Hendricks describes, a "more humane approach" in the Act of Pardon and Oblivion in 1783. Tories were allowed to keep their property. The state, however, continued to sell previously confiscated homes and land—at least until Johnston and Iredell stepped into the courtroom in 1787 and convinced a judge otherwise.[64]

The state, continued to sell previously confiscated homes and land until Johnston and Iredell convinced a judge otherwise.

The particular circumstances of *Bayard v. Singleton* were as follows. Samuel Cornell was known to be a Loyalist, and he left for England in 1775. He attempted to return to New Bern in 1777, but he refused to take an oath of loyalty. Therefore, he was forbidden to land at the port town. In an adroit effort to keep his land, Cornell deeded the land to his wife and daughter. His foresight and planning were to no avail. The state seized the property and sold it to Spyers Singleton.[65]

Johnston's argument was that the property seizure had violated his client's right to a trial by jury, as delineated in the North Carolina 1776 Constitution. The court at first wanted the two parties to settle, but neither would do so. The court then reluctantly, as historian Jeff Broadwater and author of *James Madison: A Son of Virginia and a Founder of the Nation* writes, "concluded that it could not enforce a law that was inconsistent with the constitution."[66]

The Barker House
circa 1782

Chapter Eight

EDENTON'S ROLE IN DRAFTING THE U.S. CONSTITUTION

Edenton's Hugh Williamson arrived too late to vote at the Annapolis Convention.

Many Americans believed the Articles of Confederation needed to be either revised or scrapped; the national government, in their opinion, was too weak. Calls for a revision of the Articles and calls for a new constitution were heard across the states.

Most students learn about only a few founders. Realistically, many other founders played equally or more important roles in defining the emerging nation's values.

Delegates at the Annapolis Convention, located in the convention's namesake in Maryland, agreed in September 1786 to hold a constitutional convention in Philadelphia in 1787. The purpose was to improve the Articles of Confederation and give the national government more authority. Edenton residents played a key role in the ratification debates and conventions from 1787 to 1789 and in the framing and understanding of the U.S. Constitution.

Constitutional theorist Daniel Dreisbach has argued that many Americans made significant contributions to the American Founding but are often overlooked today. Americans know how history turned out, and who held important national positions ten or twenty years after the Constitution's drafting. Our hindsight tempts us to hone in on only a few founders. This historical myopia distorts the past and prevents us from seeing the big picture. If we consider the times as they were, we will find other founders who played a critical role during the framing of the Constitution.[67]

Hugh Williamson is one example of an "other founder." Governor Richard Caswell appointed Edenton's Hugh Williamson to be a delegate at the Constitutional Convention of 1787, and he turned out to be one of the most vocal at the convention. Williamson was a Renaissance man; he was a medical doctor, an historian, and a philosopher, and his vast knowledge served him well in Philadelphia. Although other North Carolina delegates were in attendance, Williamson was the delegation's leader. The Edentonian delivered approximately 70 speeches in Independence Hall and was appointed to five committees (the second most of any delegate).[68]

One of the vocal delegates, Hugh Williamson was a Renaissance man; a medical doctor, an historian, and a philosopher. His vast knowledge served him well in Philadelphia.

A voice from Edenton was definitely heard, and

in many cases heeded, during the hot summer of 1787. Many of Williamson's ideas were incorporated into what became the supreme law of the United States—the Constitution. Here is an example. A U.S. Senator's term might be seven years had it not been for Williamson, who convinced his colleagues that a Senator's term should last only six years.

As part of what has been called the Great Compromise, Williamson and the North Carolina delegation voted for the compromise that said each state, no matter population size, would have two Senators and that state representation in the House would be based on population. Williamson wanted representation to be based solely on population, and he did not like the equality demands of the smaller states that were accustomed to more power under the Articles of Confederation. In essence, smaller states argued that every state should have the same number of representatives no matter its population. Williamson understood that "politics is the art of the possible," and he realized that a compromise was needed; if one was not reached, the smaller states might abandon the Constitution project. He no doubt persuaded the North Carolina delegation that compromise was necessary so that all state delegations signed off on the Constitution[69]

Impeachment and veto override provisions may be the most noteworthy constitutional contributions from Williamson. At the Convention, the doctor introduced the idea that the President can be impeached, and his justification and comments persuaded his peers to include an impeachment provision. Williamson also convinced delegates to include the two-thirds override provision of a presidential veto. It must be remembered, however, that Williamson

During a tour of Bartram Gardens near Philadelphia, Williamson concluded a compromise was necessary to end the 6-week debate and save the effort to produce a new constitution. The N.C. delegation later voted with small states, and the Connecticut Compromise was adopted.

(For more information see Andrea Wulf's "Founding Gardeners: The Revolutionary Generation, Nature, and the Shaping of the American Nation.")

was never for giving absolute veto power to the executive. During the debate, however, he started revising his thinking, such as an entertaining the idea for a three-quarter Congressional override. In the end, however, he encouraged the two-thirds override provision to ensure that Congress—the people's branch—maintained a significant check on the executive branch.[70]

North Carolina had five constitutional delegates: William Blount, William R. Davie, Alexander Martin, Richard Dobbs Spaight, and Hugh Williamson. Only three signed the Constitution. Hugh Williamson was among them, and he wrote often to his fellow townsmen. The other North Carolina signers were William Blount, who also later served as a territorial governor and a U.S. Senator from Tennessee, and Richard Dobbs Spaight, a future governor who died in a duel. Iredell consulted frequently via correspondence with Spaight.

In Edenton, Iredell was not only aware of the proceedings in Philadelphia, but he influenced what transpired there. He was a conduit of ideas. Spaight asked Iredell, for example, questions concerning judicial review, and Davie asked the Edentonian regarding trade regulation by the executive and judicial branches.[71]

During this period, Iredell had been nominated to run for the General Assembly. Apparently neighborhood friends, without his knowledge, had put his name in the electoral process. This would have been an important position, for the state assembly would call for a convention date to debate the merits of the proposed constitution. A Chowan County resident, Stephen Cabarrus, pledged to avoid running unless Iredell declined. Iredell eventually thanked his anonymous supporters and turned down the opportunity.

Prominent among the signers of the U.S. Constitution are North Carolina delegates Hugh Williamson (19), William Blount (18) and Richard Dobbs Spaight (17).

SCENE AT THE SIGNING OF THE CONSTITUTION OF THE UNITED STATES

1. Washington, George, Va.
2. Franklin, Benjamin, Pa.
3. Madison, James, Va.
4. Hamilton, Alexander, N.Y.
5. Morris, Gouverneur, Pa.
6. Morris, Robert, Pa.
7. Wilson, James, Pa.
8. Pinckney, Chas. Cotesworth, S.C.
9. Pinckney, Chas. S.C.
10. Rutledge, John, S.C.
11. Butler, Pierce, S.C.
12. Sherman, Roger, Conn.
13. Johnson, William Samuel, Conn.
14. McHenry, James, Md.
15. Read, George, Del.
16. Bassett, Richard, Del.
17. Spaight, Richard Dobbs, N.C.
18. Blount, William, N.C.
19. Williamson, Hugh, N.C.
20. Jenifer, Daniel of St. Thomas, Md.
21. King, Rufus, Mass.
22. Gorham, Nathaniel, Mass.
23. Dayton, Jonathan, N.J.
24. Carroll, Daniel, Md.
25. Few, William, Ga.
26. Baldwin, Abraham, Ga.
27. Langdon, John, N.H.
28. Gilman, Nicholas, N.H.
29. Livingston, William, N.J.
30. Paterson, William, N.J.
31. Mifflin, Thomas, Pa.
32. Clymer, George, Pa.
33. FitzSimons, Thomas, Pa.
34. Ingersoll, Jared, Pa.
35. Bedford, Gunning, Jr., Del.
36. Brearley, David, N.J.
37. Dickinson, John, Del.
38. Blair, John, Va.
39. Broom, Jacob, Del.
40. Jackson, William, Secretary

In 1792, nearly eighty years after the colonial capital had been established at Edenton, the new North Carolina capital was located at Raleigh.

Cabarrus then proceeded pursuing his political ambition, sought election, and soon represented Chowan constituents in the state house. He was Speaker of the House in 1789, and appointed a commission, consisting of Assemblymen, to purchase and plan a new capital for North Carolina in 1792. That new capital became Raleigh, and Cabarrus Street in downtown Raleigh is named after the Chowan countian.[72]

Chapter Nine

NORTH CAROLINA AND THE RATIFICATION PROCESS

After the Constitution had been drafted in Philadelphia, it was submitted to the people of the states to ratify. Each state called for a state ratification convention to debate the merits of the proposed Constitution. In some states, the vote was unanimous (in Georgia, 26-0, and in New Jersey, 38-0). In others a vigorous debate ensued (in Pennsylvania, 46-23, and in South Carolina, 149-73). Nine states were needed to approve the Constitution for the document to take effect. The first nine approved it rather quickly. Key states, however, remained out of the new Union: New York, North Carolina, Rhode Island, and Virginia. These states were the battleground states. The new Union needed these states, in many ways, more than the states, especially New York and Virginia, needed to be in the Union.[73]

Key states remained out of the new Union: New York, North Carolina, Rhode Island, and Virginia.

As expected, an intense debate ensued among Antifederalists and Federalists. Generally speaking, most Antifederalists refused to approve the Constitution without a Bill of Rights, a guarantee that the national government would not encroach on individual liberties and inalienable rights. The Federalists were the proponents of the Constitution, and they believed the powers given to the government were enumerated (listed) within the document. To them, a declaration of rights was unnecessary. Eventually the Federalists convinced citizens within each respective state that the Constitution should be adopted. But the road proved to be a difficult one to travel down, for many Antifederal roadblocks were placed along the way.

North Carolina was the only state to hold two ratification conventions.

The debate may have been most heated in North Carolina, where a strong Antifederalist sentiment prevailed. Edentonians and Chowan countians, including Iredell, Johnston, and Williamson—all Federalists--maneuvered in this agitated political climate. In fact, North Carolina was the only state to hold two ratification conventions: one in Hillsborough in 1788, and one in Fayetteville in 1789. In 1788, the North Carolina delegates voted (184-84) to refuse to ratify the Constitution. Antifederals and the majority of North Carolinians believed the U.S. Constitution had a glaring omission, and contrary to the arguments put forth by Federalists, opponents of the Constitution preferred an expressed guarantee of rights. To prevent the state government from encroaching on individual liberties and inalienable rights, the Fifth Provincial Congress had included a Declaration of Rights in the North Carolina Constitution of 1776. For this reason, Antifederals were befuddled as to why Federalists had omitted such a declaration from the proposed national constitution. *f* Once North Carolinians were assured in 1789 that a Bill of Rights would be added, the delegates at the Fayetteville Convention approved the document.[74]

Many of Edenton's leading citizens played a critical role in the state's transformation. Edenton's Samuel Johnston not only served as the Governor of

North Carolina from 1787 to 1789 but also served as the president of both ratification conventions. James Iredell emerged among North Carolina Federalists as the leader and spokesperson for the U.S. Constitution. He and Hugh Williamson were leading pamphleteers in the state and two of the leading political commentators in the nation. Iredell, for instance, engaged George Mason in an intellectual debate in print, and Williamson wrote one of the first pamphlets in favor of the Constitution.

James Iredell and Hugh Williamson were leading pamphleteers in North Carolina and two of the leading political commentators in the nation.

THE POWER OF THE PEN

Proponents of the Constitution had a more difficult task in North Carolina than did their Antifederal counterparts. And they knew it. So Federalists in North Carolina planned in advance and wrote essays and used contemporary media to spread their message, for many Antifederalists were popular Revolutionary War heroes and political and religious leaders who swayed public opinion.

Iredell engaged George Mason in an intellectual debate in print, and Williamson wrote one of the first pamphlets in favor of the Constitution.

In preparation for the Hillsborough convention, Federalist delegates, including James Iredell, William Davie, Hugh Williamson, William Hooper, and Archibald MacLaine, and others, wrote to each other and mailed to each other newspaper clippings and drafts of other states' convention minutes. They compared notes on the debates and other Federalist and Antifederalist essays."[75]

After Williamson's participation in drafting the U.S. Constitution in Philadelphia, he emerged as one of the first voices advocating for the Constitution's ratification. On the lawn of the Chowan County courthouse green, he more than likely spoke to Edentonians and Chowan countians on November 8, 1787, concerning the reasons for ratifying the

On the steps or the lawn of the still standing Chowan County Courthouse, political documents were often read aloud.

Constitution. While some of the first Federalist Papers essays were being drafted in New York, similar work was being done in North Carolina. Williamson's speech was later released in the form of an essay titled "Remarks on the New Plan of Government."[76]

Chowan County Courthouse

Williamson's paper advocating adoption of the new Constitution appeared in New York's "The Daily Advertiser" as the Federalist Papers were being drafted.

In February 1788, his commentary reached the Empire State, first appearing in New York City's The Daily Advertiser. It was republished subsequently in other major papers in New York, Pennsylvania, and in New Bern, North Carolina. In the end, as far north as Massachusetts and as far south as South Carolina, readers were exposed to and influenced by Williamson's ideas.[77]

Williamson is more straightforward in his essay than were Alexander Hamilton, John Jay, and James Madison in *The Federalist*. He avoids lawyerly talk and seems to be trying to reach a broader audience by discussing the benefits of joining the new proposed Union under the Constitution. Unlike the Federalist

Papers, which were answers to Antifederalist questions or counterpoints to Antifederal essays, "Remarks" is a proactive work that is an attempt to frame the debate.[78]

He argued that North Carolinians would benefit from being in the new Union, under the Constitution. Williamson points out the advantages of joining the Union, and the strengths of the Constitution and the weaknesses of the Articles of Confederation. To be more specific, North Carolina, Williamson argued, was at a geographic disadvantage compared to its neighbors in regards to ports and trade: the state should participate in a unified economy, so it could benefit from union and be economically prosperous. "Being part of something bigger, in essence," this author has written previously, "could benefit individual Tar Heels and the overall North Carolina economy." Williamson furthermore believed that the Constitution could secure liberty and property. A sincere statesman, Williamson worked for the benefit of his countrymen, not to manipulate circumstances for private gain. If he had misjudged political events and had been mistaken in his support of the Constitution, he hoped his critics "charge[d] those errors to the head, and not to the heart."[79]

During the ratification debates, Edenton's Iredell once again picked up the quill and showcased his lawyerly skill. He penned a defense of the Constitution and addressed Antifederal criticism before half of the Federalist Papers had been published. In doing so he challenged George Mason, a prominent Virginian and Constitutional Convention delegate. Mason was not simply any Antifederal. Mason had started the great Federalist/Antifederalist debate by refusing to sign the document unless it had a Bill of

Iredell penned a defense of the Constitution and addressed Antifederal criticism before half of the Federalist Papers had been published.

Rights and by later writing "Objections to the Federal Constitution." On January 8, 1788 with the pseudonym "Marcus," Iredell countered Mason's objections with *Answers to Mr. Mason's Objection to the New Constitution recommended by the late Convention at Philadelphia.* According to Willis Whichard, former North Carolina Supreme Court Justice, Dean of Campbell University Law, and biographer of James Iredell, a Norfolk printer "shelved other political tracts in 1788 to publish Iredell's 'Answers'."[80]

George Mason's objections to signing the constitution were rebutted by Edenton's Iredell.

Mason's first and primary objection was that the Constitution lacked a "Declaration of Rights," a similar concern expressed by many Tar Heel Antifederalists. A declaration of rights, he opined, was necessary, for many Americans recalled the not-so-long-ago experiences of the American Revolution and the British encroachment on liberties. Antifederalists demanded something in writing, a written contract, if you will, that guaranteed those unalienable rights. State constitutions incorporated similar declaration of rights, opponents of the Constitution quickly pointed out. So an outstanding question remained for Mason and for his compatriots in North Carolina: Why had the authors in Philadelphia excluded a declaration of rights in the proposed Constitution?[81]

Once North Carolinians were assured that a Bill of Rights would be added, the delegates at the Fayetteville Convention approved the document.

Although Iredell understood Mason's concern and argument, it was understood, he argued, that the national government could not do anything in addition to what was spelled out in the document. He and James Wilson, a future Edentonian who later sat on the same U.S. Supreme Court bench as Iredell, believed a Bill of Rights was unnecessary. In Iredell's words, "After expressly defining the powers that are to be exercised, to say that they shall exercise no other powers (either by a general or particular enumeration) would seem to me both nugatory and ridiculous." Wilson argued that a declaration of rights was dangerous; if any rights had been omitted, one might conclude that the general legislature had the authority to intervene in an individual's life and economy.[82]

Edentonians were on the cutting edge defending the Constitution, and they were aware of the Constitution's apologists in other places. Iredell had challenged Mason, and Williamson had published in papers across America. Yes, they respected and appreciated the work of Hamilton, Madison, and Jay, but they critiqued it, too. They were not in awe of their Federalist allies.

Edentonians were on the cutting edge defending the Constitution and were published in papers across America.

Charles Johnson of Strawberry Hill in Chowan County, for instance, believed the Federalist Papers to be "elegantly written" and proof of a "comprehensive imagination" and "great extent of political knowledge," but the planter believed that Federalist 13 was "wanting." It focused unnecessary attention on the benefits—economic and military—that the new Constitution offered the various states. In doing so, Alexander Hamilton suggests what separate/regional confederacies or independent states must do to thwart a foreign threat. More or less, in Johnson's mind, Publius unwittingly offered counterpoint arguments to the Antifederalists. It is always best to anticipate opposing arguments or weaknesses in your own, Johnson surmised, but do not give your opposition ammunition and ideas to counter your argument.[83]

SPEAKING ON BEHALF OF THE CONSTITUTION TO NORTH CAROLINIANS

The Hillsborough Convention convened in July

of 1788, and James Iredell emerged as the spokesperson for the Federalist cause in North Carolina. As Iredell biographer, Willis Whichard, has written: "When the Philadelphia Convention of 1787 proposed the federal Constitution, Iredell was its foremost advocate in North Carolina." He indeed was the spokesperson on the floor at Hillsborough, and he was considered the "intellectual general" of the Federalists.[84]

The opening remarks at the Hillsborough convention suggest that political opponents feared Iredell's oratory. Willie Jones, the state's leading Antifederalist, suggested delegates take an immediate vote, for they had enough time, in preparation for that day, to correspond and meet with others and reach a conclusion on the document. A delay, Antifederalists contended, meant taxpayers picked up the tab for legislator's dilly-dallying and extended session. (A more genuine concern was the Antifederals' reluctance to give Federalists a platform on which to spell out, and to do so eloquently, their points for the public record.) Iredell, however, successfully convinced his contemporaries that such an occasion as the ratification convention necessitated a lengthy and considerable debate regarding the proposed Constitution. Anything less would be a disservice to the state and to its citizens.[85]

Iredell and his counterparts, including William R. Davie, Archibald MacLaine, and William Blount, defended the Constitution from its critics.

Federalists then took the opportunity to explain, clause by clause, the Constitution. The eloquent Iredell missed no chances to persuade. Historian Pauline Maier remarks that the young lawyer "argued as if he were speaking to a jury, staying close to the point and taking care to alienate no possible ally." In hopes to end the debate sooner than later, Antifederalists remained mostly silent. Their strategy: offer little or no vocal opposition to avoid extended Federalist commentary and call for a sooner-than-later vote. Federalists, however, changed plans and took the initiative to counter Antifederalist objections that had appeared in print before the Hillsborough Convention.[86]

The delegates debated for two weeks. Iredell and his Federalist counterparts, including William R. Davie, Archibald MacLaine and William Blount, defended the Constitution from its critics, including Willie Jones of Halifax County, Samuel Spencer of Anson County, and Timothy Bloodworth of Brunswick County. For this Americans can be thankful, for the North Carolina ratification convention minutes are some of the most detailed and offer the best explanation concerning what and how the framers and ratifiers understood the Constitution.[87]

Yet after two weeks of debate, Iredell and his allies failed to convince North Carolina Antifederalists to approve the Constitution. At times, Iredell stood and explained constitutional clauses not only to end the silence in the assembly room but also to ensure that a constitutional commentary was on the public record. According to Maier, the Edenton lawyer's descriptions of the Constitution were among some of the best uttered in any of the thirteen ratification conventions. The historian especially praised Iredell's descriptions on the powers of the president and the limitations of the executive branch.[88]

Despite the lengthy commentary, the delegates voted 184 to 84 to neither reject nor ratify the Constitution.

Despite the lengthy commentary, the delegates voted 184 to 84 and refused to ratify the Constitution.

Governor Johnston and Iredell feared such an outcome, for North Carolina would remain out of the Union, at least until another state convention was called. With political animosities rekindled among

Antifederalists and Federalists, an exasperated Iredell regretted the outcome: "We are . . . for the present out of the Union, and God knows when we shall get in to it again."[89]

TO JOIN OR NOT TO JOIN?

During this American interregnum, as North Carolina was outside the new Union and essentially a distinct, sovereign entity, Federalists and North Carolinians worked to maintain good favor with the United States of America. Edenton's Hugh Williamson played an instrumental role in this regard. J. Edwin Hendricks writes, "Hugh Williamson had remained in the Confederation Congress as long as that body existed and then served as North Carolina's unofficial representative to the new government." He did not have power, but he was a spokesman for North Carolina interests in the new United States under the Constitution. His role was much like an ambassador today.[90]

Williamson penned essays to influence American opinion regarding North Carolina. Although North Carolina had genuine concerns regarding the new Constitution, Tar Heels were not enemies of their former Patriots, and Williamson stressed this point in his "Apology" (1788). Federalist critics of North Carolina had a short memory. Although the state had endured "much criticism and censure" for not adopting the Constitution, North Carolina had loaned military and provisional assistance to other invaded states during the Revolution. He then explained how North Carolina had been paying down its part of the Revolutionary war debt. How quickly proponents of the Constitution forgot these matters! Although a Federalist, who disagreed with his

Antifederal neighbors, Williamson knew that he was North Carolinians' voice and ambassador. If the other states were willing to ignore North Carolina's demands in regard to a Bill of Rights, Williamson declared, "she [North Carolina] is safest where it stands," outside the new Union.[91]

Speaking on behalf of North Carolina in New York, Williamson proved to be an excellent ambassador, for the state was starting to be recruited rather bullied into the new government. Williamson's main mission during the interregnum was to ensure that North Carolina products were not subject to any United States tariff. Thanks to Williamson's efforts, North Carolinians started to realize that the United States wanted and even needed them. Williamson's diplomatic efforts and the Virginian James Madison's promise to propose legislation in Congress for a Bill of Rights shifted public opinion in North Carolina.[92]

Before the state had approved the Constitution, George Washington had been elected as President of the United States. The Governor of North Carolina, Samuel Johnston, wrote a congratulatory note from Edenton on July 9, 1789. His opening remarks in the goodwill letter included: " Though this state be not yet a member of the union under the new form of government, we look forward with the pleasing hope of its shortly becoming such; and in the mean time consider ourselves bound in common interest and affection with other states, waiting only for the happy event of such alterations being proposed as will remove the apprehensions of many of the good citizens of this state, for those liberties for which they have fought and suffered in common with others." Johnston, and President of the Council, James Iredell, later spelled out the differences that North

Williamson proved to be an excellent ambassador, for the state was starting to be recruited rather bullied into the new government.

James Madison's promise to propose legislation in Congress for a Bill of Rights shifted public opinion about ratifying the Constitution in North Carolina.

Carolina had with other states but made sure to mention that although North Carolina differed in "some particulars in opinion" it was only in the "means of promoting them!"[93]

The "Exchange of Addresses between the Independent State of North Carolina and the Newly Elected President of the United States," reveals the importance of Edentonians in ensuring that North Carolina became part of the United States and their belief that "politics is the art of the possible." All seemed to know that their task would be a difficult one and require strategy. Williamson had worked successfully to maintain good relations between the United States and North Carolina, and Samuel Johnston and James Iredell had served their state by working to ensure public opinion shifted from Antifederal to Federal. Although they initially did not want a Bill of Rights, they conceded for its inclusion so that North Carolinians would approve (ratify) the Constitution.

The "Exchange of Addresses between the Independent State of North Carolina and the Newly Elected President of the United States" reveals the importance of Edentonians in ensuring that North Carolina became part of the United States.

Chapter Ten

EARLY INFLUENCE ON THE
U.S. SUPREME COURT

Two U.S. Supreme Court Justices, at one time or another, called Edenton home: James Iredell and James Wilson. Iredell served from 1790 to 1799, and Wilson served from 1789 to 1798. As the reader knows at this point, Iredell had been a leading Revolutionary figure, and from this port town, he created a successful law practice while influencing the state and the nation's legal and political doctrines.

Has any town other than Edenton been the residence of two U.S. Supreme Court Justices at the same time?

James Wilson

James Wilson was a leading legal figure from Pennsylvania. While serving on the U.S. Supreme Court, he moved to Edenton and lived out the remaining year of his life. Iredell and Wilson had struck up a friendship while the two sat on the national bench. "A very agreeable companion" was how Iredell described his budding friendship with the erudite justice.[94]

Born in Scotland in 1742 into a family of modest means, James Wilson later earned a scholarship to attend the University of St. Andrews. A precocious student, Wilson was influenced for a lifetime by what he learned in the halls of St. Andrews. His education would be, as historian Kermit Hall writes, his "intellectual compass." Wilson arrived in America in 1765.[95]

Not well known today, Wilson was a preeminent legal scholar and jurist in his day. During the Revolutionary War Era, and while living in Pennsylvania, he wrote pamphlets that challenged Parliamentary sovereignty (the idea that British Parliament justifiably made laws for the American colonies without the colonies being represented). He attended the Continental Congresses, and he was one of the more vocal delegates later at the 1787 Constitutional Convention. Only Madison had more influence in Philadelphia than did Wilson. Historically speaking, Wilson was in elite company: he was one of only six founders to sign both the Declaration of Independence and the Constitution.

Wilson was in elite company: he was one of only six founders to sign both the Declaration of Independence and the Constitution.

In an effort to be America's leading, legal scholar, Wilson proposed a system of law in his Lectures on Law--a series delivered to his fifteen law students at the College (now University) of Pennsylvania. While instructing nascent attorneys, he hoped one day to publish his lectures to influence and shape the general structure of American law. His lectures were eventually published, although posthumously by his son, Bird Wilson. In 1907, L. H. Alexander of Harvard University claimed that there were two great Revolutionaries, George Washington and James Wilson: the former "wielded the physical forces that made" the nation "conceived and created" in the latter's mind.[96]

Wilson possessed an insatiable appetite for fame and fortune that set up ethical lapses and financial ruin. (He had even written Lectures on Law, in part, to be famous.) Wilson was a land speculator, whose financial endeavors often failed. He acquired more debt to repay the loans for capital for failed investments in land speculation. He was trapped in an inescapable cycle of debt.[97]

Meanwhile, as an Associate Justice, like Iredell, on the U.S. Supreme Court, Wilson desired to be Chief Justice. When John Jay resigned from the bench in 1795 (he had been elected Governor of New York), Wilson expected to be the next Chief Justice. George Washington, however, overlooked Wilson, and nominated Oliver Ellsworth. A brilliant Wilson was baffled. How could the President, in Wilson's mind, overlook the best legal theorist in the United States?[98]

The first President may have anticipated Wilson's arrest and imprisonment for debt in July 1797. (Wilson went down in history, to this date, as the only Supreme Court Justice to have been incarcerated.) After being released from prison, Wilson, a Pennsylvanian, headed south to live in Edenton. While there, a creditor in South Carolina demanded payment, but Wilson remained broke. The Associate Justice ended up behind bars once again. The creditor

Historian L.H. Alexander said of George Washington and James Wilson: the former "wielded the physical forces that made" the nation "conceived and created" in the latter's mind.

To this date, James Wilson is the only U.S. Supreme Court Justice to have been incarcerated.

soon overlooked Wilson's debt, and the jurist was released from jail.

Practically a fugitive from pursuing creditors, the scholar lived out his remaining days, with rapidly increasing stress and declining health in Edenton at the Horniblow Tavern. After his death in 1798, Wilson's family lacked the money to return his body to Philadelphia for a burial. He was therefore buried in the Johnston Cemetery at Hayes Plantation. His body was exhumed in 1906, and he was reinterred at Christ Church in Philadelphia.[99]

During his lifetime, Wilson acquired fame but not the kind he had hoped for. Few offered any positive comments regarding his life, for at the time, he was mostly remembered for his massive debt and ethical lapses. Iredell, and apparently Samuel Johnston, however, had a soft spot for Wilson, and they had often worried about his declining health and its effect on his young wife. After Wilson's death, Iredell helped Wilson's son settle his father's estate, and helped Wilson's wife settle financial affairs in Edenton.[100]

IREDELL GOES TO COURT

James Iredell was appointed to the U.S. Supreme Court in 1790.

Wilson's Supreme Court colleague, James Iredell, was appointed to the Court in 1790 as recognition for his efforts to ratify the Constitution and for his legal prowess. As did other Federalists on the bench, Iredell worked to preserve and strengthen the nascent national government that he had helped to create. Iredell promoted a federal form of government, however. As Whichard states: "While virtually rabid in his federalism, Iredell had an equally passionate commitment to the concept of dual sovereignty and perceived no incongruity between the two." In other words, the Associate Justice believed the Constitution, Whichard explains, did not "interfere with the internal regulations of a state in matters that concerned the state only."[101]

On the Supreme Court bench, Iredell continued writing essays. His most famous, albeit anonymous ones, were "A Citizen of Pennsylvania" and "To the Citizens of the United States." In both he defended President Washington's policies. In the former, he defended the excise tax on distilled spirits—the tax that led Pennsylvania farmers to revolt and what historians call the Whiskey Rebellion of 1794. In Iredell's mind, an excise tax on a non-essential was better than a direct tax affecting everyone. He defended Washington's suppression of Pennsylvania farmers with the help of approximately 15,000 militiamen: Iredell's defense, according to Whichard, was that the "well-being of every state and every individual was inseparably interwoven with that of the Union." The Union's survival depended on the people's trust in the newly formed government, so Washington was justified to put down the farmer's revolt against excise taxes.[102]

It was not uncommon for Hannah Iredell to attend presidential functions, or for her husband to dine with George Washington.

During Washington's two terms, he and Iredell struck up a companionship. It was not uncommon for Hannah Iredell to attend presidential functions, or for her husband to dine with George Washington. While in office, Washington wrote to Iredell when he was on circuit or in Edenton, and when Washington wanted to tour the South in his first term, he asked Iredell for suggested stopping points for his presidential tour. One recommendation turned out to be a lukewarm reception. Still sour from losing the overall ratification debate, former Antifederalist Willie Jones, when notified of Washington's itinerary, let it be known that he would meet George Washington as a general and as a man, but not as his President.[103]

As a Supreme Court jurist, the Edentonian is most known for his decisions in *Calder v. Bull* (1798) and *Chisholm v. Georgia* (1793).

In *Calder v. Bull,* Iredell, as well as the majority of the court, ruled that the *ex post facto* doctrine applied only to criminal cases. It did not apply to civil cases. (*Ex post facto* means "after the fact"--passing a law making behavior before the law's passage illegal.) *Calder v. Bull* also prompted a centuries long legal debate whether natural law is a "valid reference point for judicial review of legislative enactments." Justices Chase and Iredell disagreed, and ever since the decision, justices have cited or echoed the two's opposing views. (See footnote for further explanation).[104]

In *Chisholm v. Georgia,* Iredell cast the lone dissenting opinion. In 1793, Alexander Chisholm, an executor of a South Carolina estate, sued the state of Georgia for not making payments on received supplies. The court ruled (4-1) that a disagreement between a state and citizens of another state fell under the federal court's authority, and the Supreme Court could review a state's conduct. Hearkening back to his arguments put forth at the Hillsborough ratification convention and to English common law, Iredell disagreed with the majority. His dissent ultimately provided the blueprint for the Eleventh Amendment: "The judicial power of the United States shall not be construed to extend to any suit in law or equity, commenced or prosecuted against one of the United States by citizens of another state, or by citizens or subjects of any foreign state."[105]

When Chief Justice John Jay resigned in 1795,

George Washington considered a few potential candidates to head the Supreme Court. He eventually set his sights on Iredell. Arthur Iredell more than likely sighed relief, for he considered his brother, not James Wilson, to be the best legal mind in America. And therein lay the dilemma for Washington. He preferred Iredell, but Wilson was the Edentonian's senior on the bench. In the end, Washington nominated and the Senate approved Oliver Ellsworth as Chief Justice. Ever the diplomat, Iredell understood the President's dilemma, and whatever his thoughts, the Associate Justice never expressed negative ones in public.[106]

Edenton's own, U.S. Supreme Court Justice, James Iredell died in 1799.

In the 1790s, the Supreme Court Justices traveled frequently to hear cases, and the itinerancy took its toll on Iredell's health. He died in 1799. After his death, unlike Wilson, he was remembered fondly. Known as a kind man, many remarked on his "goodness" and "benevolence." Bishop Charles Pettigrew of St. Paul's Church described Iredell as "so humane, so sympathetic, so charitable, so humble, and so easy of access."[107]

Iredell has a lasting constitutional and judicial legacy. Influential historian Bernard Bailyn once described the Edentonian as "one of the most penetrating minds among the federalists." Felix Frankfurter, an Associate Justice on the Supreme Court (1939-1962), considered Iredell's arguments and his Supreme Court decisions as witness to a "man of talent" and "one of the really brilliant minds of his period, if not of our entire history."[108]

The Barker House
Circa 1782

Conclusion

As I sit outside the Barker House and look over Albemarle Sound and hear the birds flying overhead, I must remind myself that during the 1770s, I would have seen numerous ship masts and sails on the water and heard the call of sailors and captains at the docks. I would have seen fishermen, black and white, dropping nets into the Albemarle waters or bringing their massive catches of herring into port. I might have heard Edentonians making contracts with fellow townsmen for repair work, or mason work, or blacksmithing. I would have seen white farmers and free blacks and slaves driving wagons of tobacco and other crops into town to be stored in one of the many warehouses before being shipped elsewhere in America or overseas. I may have even seen a sailor walking back from town, from the ropewalk, with smaller cords to be used on his vessel, or others hauling larger, coiled ropes on wagons to the docks.

As I step inside the 1767 historic courthouse, it is quiet, and I hear my footsteps echo off the walls as I walk over the stone floor. With some historical imagination, I can hear James Iredell and Samuel Johnston making cogent arguments across the bar, and as I turn around and look outside the front courthouse door, I can imagine prestigious locals such as Thomas Jones and Thomas Benbury in attendance. As I look across the verdant courthouse lawn, I think back to Daniel Earl's "Resolutions," and I imagine an excited assembly listening to the "Resolutions" being read aloud or listening and pondering when other political pamphlets were read aloud. (Where did "Parson Earl" find the time to be so politically active, pastor a church, and run successful businesses?)

As I walk along the sidewalks in town, I imagine Samuel Johnston and John Harvey walking, possibly to Joseph Hewes's house, discussing the news and formulating political strategy. In their homes by the sunlight through the window by day or by candlelight or fireplace light by night, I imagine Edentonians dipping quills into inkwells and penning letters on parchment regarding the recent developments in town and in Philadelphia. I imagine hearing different accents—English, Scottish, Irish, and French—as the letters are proofread aloud before being mailed. I imagine literate Edentonians, outside a tavern, reading newspapers brought from Suffolk and discussing hot political topics with their semi-literate neighbors. When I later step into St. Paul's Church, I wonder what it must have been like in 1776. Were parishioners strictly focused on worship or did the sermon turn into a political harangue?

Indeed, Edenton and Chowan County were flourishing and comprised a bustling hub, economically and politically. The town was home to the first organized political activity by women in the American colonies, and it was home to a signatory of the Declaration of Independence and the Constitution. Governors of North Carolina called the town home, and a Speaker of the North Carolina House and persons instrumental in the drafting of the first state constitution and its declaration of rights called Chowan County home. Some of the state's and nation's greatest legal minds hailed from the area, and their ideas were spread across the nation in print. Also, two Justices of the United States Supreme Court resided in Edenton.

When walking in "The South's Prettiest Small Town" and admiring the architectural gems near the cresting, small waves of the Albemarle Sound, one should also appreciate that Edentonians put the town and surrounding area on the map as an intellectual capital and economic and political hub of the early United States.

The Barker House
circa 1782

Timeline of Important Events:

Purpose: The timeline provides readers with a sense of the colonial history of Edenton up to the Founding Era. It also offers readers historical context and a glimpse into how the town fits into overall British colonial history in North America and what later became known as North Carolina and the United States. It sets the stage for the story that is told in *The King's Trouble Makers: Edenton's Role in Creating a Nation and State*.

1492—Christopher Columbus finds what Europeans call the New World.

1584—Approximately 1,200 coastal miles in the "New World" are named Virginia.

1585—England's first colony is established on the Outer Banks at Roanoke Island.

1586—The British further explore the Albemarle Sound and the Chowan and Roanoke Rivers.

1590—John White finds Roanoke colony abandoned.

1607—Jamestown (Virginia) is established.

1619—The first black Africans arrive in Jamestown as indentured servants and have the same opportunities as white indentured servants who arrived in the decade following English settlement of Jamestown. These opportunities lasted until slave laws were passed in Virginia in the 1660s.

1620—Pilgrims land at Plymouth in what becomes the Massachusetts Bay colony.

1642-49—A civil war occurs in England. Events will influence Great Britain's politics in the American colonies during the latter part of the 1600s and during the 1700s.

1650—Europeans start to settle the Albemarle region (more or less modern-day northeastern North Carolina).

1657—Nathaniel Batts settles on land near the western part of the Albemarle Sound.

1660—Charles II is restored to the English Crown.

1663—Charles II rewards some of his political allies with land grants. The Eight Proprietors of Carolina (modern-day North Carolina and South Carolina) are awarded land grants.

--- The Carolina Charter is written.

1665—Concessions and Agreement is written. The document implemented the provisions in the 1663 Carolina Charter and created a court system, a unicameral legislature, and a system of tax collection.

1668—Chowan, Currituck, Pasquotank, and Perquimans precincts are formed.

1669—Proprietors approve the Fundamental Constitutions of Carolina.

1701—St. Paul's Church (in modern-day Edenton) is organized.

1712—The Town of Queen Anne's Creek (later named Edenton) begins after passage of an Act of Assembly in that year.

--- Carolina is separated into North and South.

--- Edward Hyde was commissioned governor of North Carolina by the Lords Proprietors. He died the same year and had little influence in this position.

--- Freed slave families from Norfolk County, Virginia are deeded land in Chowan County.

1712-1719—Precinct Court is held in the homes of town residents.

1713-22—Charles Eden is appointed governor of North Carolina. He was appointed in 1713 and assumed all gubernatorial responsibilities the following year. He brought order to an unruly North Carolina and served as governor until his death in 1722.

1715—North Carolina colony passes law encouraging the construction of a courthouse in the "metropolis of the Albemarle," that was later called Edenton.

1716—Chief Justice Christopher Gale holds first court session at the "Courthouse Queen Anne's Creek." Town emerges as the political center of the Albemarle region and the colony. As a result, many visit the town for legal matters. Its location encourages merchant activity and Edenton evolves as a port town.

1719—The first courthouse, in what would become known as Edenton, was constructed and in use. It was a wooden building.

1722—Town of Queen Anne's Creek, also known as the Port of Roanoke, is named for Governor Eden and is called Edenton.

1723--Robert Hicks deeds 50 acres to Commissioners of Edenton. Edenton commissioners sell lots to Justices of Chowan County for a new courthouse to be built. Never built.

1728—Surveyors mark the North Carolina-Virginia boundary line.

--- William Byrd II of Virginia visits Edenton.

1729—George II purchases land from seven of the eight Lord Proprietors.

1734—Vestry of St. Paul's meets in Chowan County courthouse.

1736—The existing structure of St. Paul's Church is constructed.

1737—The last year the General Assembly met exclusively in Edenton. The legislative body alternated assemblies between Edenton and New Bern for the next seven years.

1738—An Act to Erect a Gaol in Edenton is adopted.

1739—The last year that the General Court met exclusively in Edenton. The court was the colony's equivalent to a modern-day state Supreme Court.

1743—The last time the General Assembly convened in Edenton.

1749—William Bonner moves warehouses closer to town wharves

to meet demand for increasing trade.

1752—Bishop August Gottlieb Spangenburg visits Edenton to meet with Francis Corbin, Lord Granville's land agent, to purchase land for a Moravian settlement, later called Wachovia in the Piedmont of North Carolina.

1754-1763—The Seven Years War occurs. Americans call it The French and Indian War. During the turmoil, Americans and British combated England's European and continental archenemy, France, and the various Indian tribes within the American colonies. Some historians have considered this war to be the first global war.

1755—Richard Brownrigg buys a tract of Chowan County land, and Wingfield emerges as a bustling shipping point beside the Chowan River, where fishermen were known to bring in hundreds of barrels of shad and herring in one hour.

1758—The Cupola House is built in Edenton, where it still stands.

1759—A couple dozen horsemen from Halifax County abduct Francis Corbin, land agent, and take him back to the town of Enfield. Under duress, he promised to disclose his office's records. This incident has become known as the Enfield Riot.

1764—Sugar Act is passed by the British Parliament. It is a part of an effort to ensure that American colonists repaid the expenses incurred by the British government to protect Americans during the Seven Years War and for any future protection.

1765—British Parliament passes the Stamp Act and the Quartering Act. The former irritated many American colonists, who protested its existence.

   --- Sons of Liberty group forms in Edenton.

1766—British Parliament repeals the Stamp Act. Americans start to realize that protests can serve as a means to accomplish political goals.

1767—Historic Chowan County Courthouse is constructed. It is still in use today.

1769—The Sauthier map of Edenton is drawn.

1770—Edenton Academy is chartered.

1768-1771—Regulator Rebellion occurs in North Carolina. Piedmont farmers clash with stern North Carolinians and the militia.

--- Samuel Johnston plays a critical role in putting down the Regulators.

1771—The Battle of Alamance occurs and the Regulator Rebellion ends.

1772—Joseph Pilmore, an influential Methodist itinerant, preaches in Edenton.

1773—Boston Tea Party occurs.

North Carolina forms a Committee of Correspondence to coordinate with other colonies responses to Great Britain. Among its nine members are four from the Albemarle region: John Harvey of Perquimans County, Edward Vail of Chowan County, Samuel Johnston of Chowan County, and Joseph Hewes of Edenton.

1774—Led by Penelope Barker, women in Edenton and Chowan County protest the Tea Act in an event that has become known as the Edenton Tea Party.

--- Benedict Arnold's ship docked at Edenton.

--- James Iredell's To The Inhabitants of Great Britain is published.

--- First Provincial Congress is held. Delegates across North Carolina meet to discuss what should be done regarding what they consider encroachments on their liberties and violations of colonial charters.

1775—John Harvey of Perquimans County calls for a Second Provincial Congress.

--- On March 31, the Mecklenburg Resolves are issued.

--- Second Provincial Congress is held from April 3-7.

--- Edenton's James Iredell pens Principles of an American Whig.

--- Third Provincial Congress is held from August

20-September 10.

--- Joseph Hewes of Edenton is one of three North Carolinians representing the colony at the First Continental Congress in Philadelphia.

--- Masonic Lodge is formed in Edenton.

--- Chowan County Committee of Safety enforces the non-importation of British goods.

--- John Harvey dies and Samuel Johnston emerges as the Albemarle's and North Carolina's leading Revolutionary.

1776—Fourth Provincial Congress meets in Halifax. By a unanimous vote (81-0) delegates pass the Halifax Resolves, a resolution that empowers NC delegates at the Continental Congress in Philadelphia to work with delegates from other colonies to declare independence from Great Britain, if deemed necessary.

--- Delegates from thirteen colonies sign Declaration of Independence. It is commemorated on July 4th.

--- Fifth Provincial Congress meets from November 12 to December 23.

--- On December 18, the first North Carolina Constitution is approved. Edenton's residents played a key part.

1777—Richard Caswell is elected first Governor of North Carolina as an independent state.

--- Dr. Hugh Williamson chooses to live in Edenton.

--- The Articles of Confederation is introduced to states to ratify.

1778—Masons of Unanimity Lodge meet in 1767 Chowan County courthouse.

1779—Joseph Hewes dies.

--- Town is threatened by British for first time.

1780—Town is again under threat of British attack. No attack occurs. Approximately 35 miles west of Edenton, General Thomas Benbury and 1,200 militiamen were positioned at Norfleet's Mill to thwart a possible British attack.

1781—Lord Cornwallis surrenders at Yorktown, Virginia.

A British ship takes an American schooner and a ship off waters of Edenton. In a makeshift flotilla—a barge, two boats, and a canoe—Edentonians retake the captured ship. The British, however, burned the schooner.

--- All thirteen states approved Articles of Confederation.

1783—Treaty of Paris officially ends the conflict, also known as the Revolutionary War, between Great Britain and the American colonists.

--- Francis Asbury, a leading Methodist evangelist, preaches a sermon in Edenton.

--- Samuel Johnston presides over meeting held at the courthouse. Attendees discuss the new nation's future.

--- Josiah Collins, Sr. purchases a ropewalk (facility for making rope) in Edenton. It remains open until 1839.

1787-1789—Samuel Johnston of Chowan County serves as North Carolina's governor.

1787—U.S. Constitution is drafted in Philadelphia by 55 delegates from what were the various American colonies.

--- Bayard v. Singleton is heard. The court case is one of the first in which a court declared a law unconstitutional.

1788—A state ratification convention is held in Hillsborough. Delegates voted to neither reject nor approve the Constitution.

--- James Iredell, Sr. emerges as the leading Federalist in North Carolina.

--- Hugh Williamson of Edenton publishes his "Apology" in the New York Daily Advertiser.

1789-1793—Samuel Johnston serves as one of North Carolina's first United States senators.

1789—North Carolina approves U.S. Constitution at Fayetteville ratification convention and joins the union formed under the Constitution.

--- All states (except for Rhode Island) approve U.S. Constitution.

--- February celebration is held in Edenton for George

Washington's birthday.

1790—Dismal Swamp Canal charter is approved.

--- James Wilson is nominated for U.S. Supreme Court.

1791—George Washington tours towns in North Carolina.
President solicited recommendations from James Iredell,
Sr. of Edenton.

--- James Iredell of Edenton is eventually nominated by
Washington to the U.S. Supreme Court and is confirmed
by the U.S. Senate.

1792—New state capital site is called Raleigh, in honor of Sir
Walter Raleigh.

1793— Iredell's lone dissent in Chisholm v. Georgia inspires a call
for an amendment to the U.S. Constitution. The 11th
Amendment overturned the majority's ruling that included
future Edentonian James Wilson's opinion.

1794—General Assembly starts meeting in Raleigh.

1795—The University of North Carolina opens its doors to
students.

1798—U.S. Supreme Court Justice James Wilson dies a debtor. He
is buried in Edenton.

1799—U.S. Supreme Court Justice James Iredell dies.

--- The North Carolina—Tennessee border is finalized.

List of Historical Characters:

PENELOPE BARKER (1728-1796)

The leader of what has become known as the Edenton Tea Party (1774), the first organized political act by women in what became the United States. The event made international news. Penelope married three times. Her first two husbands died, and she inherited their wealth. Her third husband, Thomas Barker, was Treasurer for the Northern District of North Carolina from 1748 to 1764, and he represented North Carolina as an agent in London during the 1760s and 1770s.

THOMAS BENBURY (1736-1793)

A judge, planter, and vestryman at St. Paul's Church in Edenton, Benbury emerged as a staunch Patriot during the Revolutionary War. He was a delegate at all five North Carolina Provincial Congresses, and he served on Edenton's Committee of Safety, a post that he held with utmost vigilance and one in which William Hooper criticized his Patriot enthusiasm. He was a brigadier general during the Revolutionary War, and President George Washington appointed him Collector of Customs for Port of Edenton.

TIMOTHY BLOODWORTH (1736-1814)

An autodidact and farmer from Brunswick County and a Patriot who helped form the Wilmington Committee of Safety in 1775. He was elected to Congress in 1784 and resigned from the post in 1787. He was an outspoken Antifederalist at the Hillsborough and Fayetteville conventions—North Carolina's two ratification conventions—and he was a leading Tar Heel critic of the proposed Constitution who questioned James Iredell's reasons for adopting the document. Even so, he was elected to the U.S. House in 1790, and to the U.S. Senate in 1795.

WILLIAM BLOUNT (1749-1800)

A Bertie County native and delegate to the 1787 Constitutional Convention and signer of the U.S. Constitution, Blount ended his political career in scandalous fashion. During the ratification debates, he promoted the approval of the Constitution. With a cumbersome job title, he later served as Governor of the Territory of the United States South of the Ohio River and negotiated the Treaty of Holston—a document in which the Cherokee ceded land to the U.S. He played an instrumental role in the creation of the state of Tennessee and in its first constitution. He later served as a U.S. Senator for the Volunteer State, but he was later expelled from the Senate for plotting to help the British take Florida, New Orleans, and Louisiana from the Spanish.

STEPHEN CABARRUS (1754-1808)

The Frenchman moved to Edenton and later became a North Carolina notable, maybe in part because he married a rich and established woman, seventeen years his senior. He was a Federalist, a proponent of the U.S. Constitution, and served as a delegate to North Carolina's two ratification conventions. He served in the North Carolina House of Commons (1784-1805) and frequently served as its Speaker. He was a Trustee of the University of North Carolina. Cabarrus Street in downtown Raleigh is named for him.

RICHARD CASWELL (1729-1789)

The Maryland native gained respect among his colleagues in his new home, North Carolina. He served in the colonial assembly from 1754-76, and he served as speaker in 1769. It was during this time that Caswell promoted educational reform: each county should have a free-school. He was a delegate to all five North Carolina Provincial Congresses and to the First and Second Continental Congresses. Although Caswell avoided espousing Patriot viewpoints preceding the Revolutionary War, he worked surreptitiously for American independence. In particular, he worked to obtain government records and the treasury. With official records and money, North Carolina, it was believed, did not need England. He participated at the Battle of Moore's Creek Bridge in 1776 and was later elected the first governor of the independent state of North Carolina. He served in this capacity from 1776-1780, the year in which he became a major general. In 1785, he was reelected governor and served until 1788. As governor, he was known as a natural leader and a coalition builder.

JOSIAH COLLINS, SR. (1735-1819)

A native of England, Collins arrived in Edenton in 1777 and became a successful merchant. One of his more noteworthy business pursuits was purchasing a ropewalk from Joseph Hewes. This most likely business in a port town lasted from 1783 and under his son's management until 1839. Collins's ropes were used as cords on boats and netting for seine fishing. As the shipbuilding industry grew, so did Collins's fortune. Collins was also a land speculator, and his Lake Company brought over slaves to build canals. By 1800, Lake Company was valued at $200,000. He purchased approximately 25,000 acres in Tennessee and purchased what became known as Somerset Plantation, originally owned by the Lake Company until Collins bought out his business partners. It was bequeathed to is son, Josiah Collins II.

JOSIAH COLLINS, II (1763-1829)

A merchant, planter, and banker, Collins, successfully ran his father's Edenton rope factory. He helped organize the Episcopal Diocese of North Carolina while owning one of the largest plantations in North Carolina—Somerset Plantation.

FRANCIS CORBIN (DIED 1767)

Lord Granville was the only land proprietor out of the eight, who refused to sell land back to the English Crown. Francis Corbin was his land agent from 1744 to 1759. Corbin operated a land office out of one of his houses, the Cupola House in Edenton. Eventually he lost favor with notable Carolinians and Lord Granville, who relinquished him of his duties after Royal Governor Arthur Dobbs accused Corbin of illegally granting Granville's land. Corbin, however, was shortly thereafter elected by Chowan countians to represent them in the General Assembly.

WILLIAM R. DAVIE (1756-1820)

A College of New Jersey (Princeton) graduate and a wounded Revolutionary War veteran and general, Davie later represented North Carolina at the 1787 Constitutional Convention in Philadelphia and emerged as one of North Carolina's leading Federalists during the ratification debates. He has been considered the Founder of the University of North Carolina. He was Grand Master of the Masons in North Carolina (1792-98), and he was elected governor of North Carolina in 1798.

DANIEL EARL (DIED 1790)

The rector of St. Paul's Church possessed an entrepreneurial mindset. He arrived in Chowan County in 1757 and built a plantation, named Bandon. He was known for improving weaving and loom methods and for his herring fisheries. Some parishioners believed Earl should be less an entrepreneur and more of a shepherd to his flock. Earl supported the American Revolution and resigned as rector of St. Paul's in 1778.

CHARLES EDEN (1673-1722)

The last person to hold a landgrave title in the feudal-like proprietorship system in North Carolina was Charles Eden. In 1713, Queen Anne appointed him to be Governor of North Carolina, and his term lasted from 1714 to 1722. The governor brought order to an unruly colony, yet he allegedly colluded with pirates such as Edward Teach, also known as Blackbeard.

CORNELIUS HARNETT, JR. (1723-1781)

The Wilmingtonian was a leading Patriot, who died for his beliefs during the Revolutionary War. He also served in several local public offices such as the Wilmington town commission (1750). He served as a representative in the colonial assembly (1754- 1776). After Parliament passed the Stamp Act (1765), he emerged as chairman of the Sons of Liberty in Wilmington and a leader protesting what he deemed encroachment on individual liberty. In 1775, he was the President of the Provincial Council of Safety, a position that effectively made him the chief executive of the evolving state government. In 1781, the British captured the Patriot and imprisoned him. In declining health, he soon died after his incarceration.

JOHN HARVEY (1724-1775)

Many North Carolinians considered the Perquimans County resident to be the leading North Carolina revolutionary. Samuel Johnston of Chowan County assumed that role when Harvey passed a way a year before the colonies withdrew from Great Britain. His political career began at 21 as a member of the General Assembly. He was a longstanding representative of Perquimans County. He was at the vanguard for revolution in the mid-1770s. He was Moderator of the North Carolina First Provincial Congress, and he called for the Second Provincial Congress.

JOSEPH HEWES (1730-1779)

A resident of Edenton and a signer of the Declaration of Independence, Hewes was a leading merchant in the port town, and he started a ropewalk that was later sold to Josiah Collins, Sr. Although he moved to Edenton without knowing anyone, he soon was respected and influential. He served in the colonial assembly from 1760-1774, and he was a delegate to the Continental Congress (1774-1777). He served in the Fifth Provincial Congress, the assembly that drafted the first state constitution. During the Revolutionary War, he served on the Naval Board as its Secretary; all communication went through him. In 1777, fellow North Carolinian and signer of the Declaration of Independence, John Penn, accused Hewes of holding multiple offices and using his position for personal profit. Disappointed and offended, Hewes retired that year. In 1779, he retired from his newly elected position in the Continental Congress. He died two weeks later.

WILLIAM HOOPER (1742-1790)

The Harvard College graduate and Wilmingtonian was one of North Carolina's three signers of the Declaration of Independence. He was a leading Revolutionary and corresponded frequently with fellow pamphleteer James Iredell, Sr. He was also a well-respected attorney, who had studied under James Otis. He served on North Carolina's Committee of Correspondence. He was one of the youngest delegates at the First and Second Continental Congresses, and he served at four of the five Provincial Congress in North Carolina. His political influence lessened in the latter years of his life.

JAMES IREDELL, SR. (1751-1799)

The Edenton resident became one the first Justices on the United States Supreme Court (1791-99). Prior to this position, he was a successful attorney who had served as a North Carolina Superior Court judge (1777-78) and State attorney general (1779-81). He played a role for the defense in *Bayard v. Singleton* (1787), a famous case that had national importance and introduced the concept of judicial review. Iredell was also a skillful orator and persuasive Founding Era pamphleteer.

CHARLES JOHNSON (DIED 1802)

A Scotland native, he married Parson Daniel Earl's daughter, Elizabeth. Like many Edentonians, Johnson was a Federalist during the ratification debates. He had served in the state senate (1781-84, 1789). In the year North Carolina ratified the Constitution (1789), Johnson was Speaker of the North Carolina Senate. He had a brief tenure in the U.S. Congress, and he served from 1801 until his death.

SAMUEL JOHNSTON (1733-1816)

The native of Scotland soon became one of North Carolina's and the nation's leading politicians during the first days of the United States of America. A successful attorney, he held numerous political offices including a long tenure in the General Assembly (1759-75) and three terms as the state's governor (1787-89). He served as president of the Third and Fourth Provincial Congresses. As a delegate to the Continental Congress in 1780, he was elected as president of that body; he declined the offer. In *Bayard v. Singleton* (1787), he represented a Loyalist who had had property seized by the state government during the Revolutionary War. The Chowan countian was North Carolina's First Grand Master of the Masons, and he served as a U.S. Senator from 1789 to 1793. He eventually moved to Martin County and worked as a Superior Court judge (1800-1803). He was a Trustee of the University of North Carolina.

THOMAS JONES (DIED 1797)

A good friend of James Iredell, Sr., Jones corresponded with one of the first Justices of the U.S. Supreme Court on a regular basis. The 1776 North Carolina constitution—the state's first constitution—

has been referred to as "Jones's constitution," for he played an instrumental role in its drafting at the Fifth Provincial Congress. He was also on the committee at the Fourth Provincial Congress that drafted the Halifax Resolves, and he served on the Provincial Council.

WILLIE JONES (1741-1801)

Jones was one of the largest slaveholders and real property owners in the state of North Carolina, and he emerged as a leading Antifederalist during the ratification debates. Although he disagreed with Richard Caswell and Samuel Johnston later in regards to the Constitution, he had allied with them when putting down the Regulator Rebellion (1768-1771). He attended four of the five Provincial Congresses, and later proved to be an influential state politician in the House of Commons (1777-1780) and as a state Senator (1782, 84, and 88). He voiced the strongest opposition to the adoption of the U.S. Constitution, for it had no Bill of Rights as originally submitted to the thirteen state ratification conventions. As a committee member in 1792, he helped plan the City of Raleigh. Jones Street in downtown Raleigh is named for him.

ARCHIBALD MACLAINE (1728-1790)

An Irish native, MacLaine later became a successful Wilmington merchant and attorney. He was a leader in the Stamp Act protest (1765-66). He later served on Wilmington's Committee of Safety. In 1776, he served on the committee at the Fifth Provincial Congress that wrote the North Carolina Constitution and its declaration of rights. Even so, many had accused him of Tory sympathies, for his step-son was indeed a Loyalist during the Revolutionary War. During the ratification debates (1787-89), he was a Federalist who penned essays under the pseudonym "Publicola." He was a Trustee of the University of North Carolina.

JOHN PENN (1740-1788)

The Granville countian was one of North Carolina's three signers of the Declaration of Independence. He was also a delegate at the Continental Congress (1775) and a delegate to the Third and Fourth Provincial Congresses in North Carolina. As a delegate at the Continental Congress, he attended more sessions than any other delegate. A few years later Edentonian Joseph Hewes alleged that Penn neglected his responsibilities. Penn served on North Carolina's Board of War until 1781 and as President of the Governor's Council.

JAMES WILSON (1742-1798)

One of the first justices on the U.S. Supreme Court and an Edenton resident the last year of his life, Wilson was in a select group: one of only six Americans to sign the Declaration of Independence and the U.S. Constitution. He was one of the most influential members of the 1787 Constitutional Convention in Philadelphia. In an unfortunate series of events, however, Wilson was the only Supreme Court justice to be imprisoned. He died a debtor in Edenton.

Sources: Biographical information (all but one listing) is from William S. Powell's magisterial *Dictionary of North Carolina Biography, Vol. 1 – 6* (Chapel Hill, 1979 – 1996). James Wilson's information is taken from Kermit L. Hall and Mark David Hall, eds., *Collected Works of James Wilson, Vol. I* (Indianapolis, 2007).

Endnotes

[1] Inglis Fletcher, *Queen's Gift.* (Indianapolis, 1952), 6, and Marc D. Brodsky, *The Courthouse at Edenton: A History of the Chowan County Courthouse of 1767* (Edenton, 1989), 37.

[2] The Provincial Congress was a colonial legislative body similar to what is now a state legislature. The Continental Congress was an assembly that included delegates from all the American colonies.

[3] Federalists were supporters of a stronger national government with enumerated powers, yet they wanted the states to retain sovereignty in many other matters.

[4] *Novus Ordo Seclorum* is a Latin phrase that is included as part of the Great Seal of the United States. It also appears on the one-dollar bill.

[5] Dr. Richard Dillard and Capt. Richard Dixon, eds., *A Brief History of Edenton and Its Environs* (Elizabeth City, n.d.) and William S. Powell, *North Carolina Through Four Centuries* (Chapel Hill, 1989), 73.

[6] Powell, *North Carolina*, 78, 104-13.

[7] Milton Ready, *The Tar Heel State: A History of North Carolina* (Columbia, S.C., 2005), 44-47.

[8] Powell, *North Carolina*, 105; Ready, *Tar Heel State*, 50-51.

[9] Brodsky, *Courthouse at Edenton*, 19-21.

[10] Robert L. Ganyard, The Emergence of North Carolina's Revolutionary State Government (Raleigh, 1978), 6-7 and Powell,

North Carolina, 93-95.

[11] Brodsky, *Courthouse at Edenton*, 20. Lords Proprietors were eight men to whom the Crown had given large tracks of land as rewards for their political loyalty.

[12] Powell, *North Carolina*, 105, 112.

[13] Troy Kickler, "Joseph Hewes," *NorthCarolinahistory.org: An Online Encyclopedia*, North Carolina History Project, http://www. northcarolinahistory.org/encyclopedia/442/entry (accessed July 1, 2013); Kellie Slappey, "Daniel Earl," *NorthCarolinahistory.org: An Online Encyclopedia*, North Carolina History Project, http://www. northcarolinahistory.org/encyclopedia/467/entry (accessed July 1, 2013); Ganyard, *Emergence*, 5.

[14] Thomas C. Parramore, *Cradle of the Colony: The History of Chowan County and Edenton, North Carolina* (Edenton, 1967).

[15] Brodsky, *Courthouse at Edenton*, 20-24, 32-35, 37. A ropewalking operation acquired this description because a worker actually walked backward, feeding hemp yarn, to a wheel on the other end that twisted the yarn into rope. Ropewalkers made ropes and cords of various dimensions. Some roperies could be as long as a quarter of a mile. (For more on ropewalking see George Stevenson, "Ropewalks" in William S. Powell, ed., *Encyclopedia of North Carolina* (Chapel Hill, 2006) and Mathew Schaffer, "Edenton Ropewalk" *NorthCarolinahistory.org: An Online Encyclopedia*, North Carolina History Project, http://www.northcarolinahistory.org/ encyclopedia/
entry/896 (accessed August 22, 2013).

[16] Larry Schweikart and Michael Allen, *A Patriot's History of the United States* (New York, 2004), 54-64; Brendan McConville, "Revolutionary War" in Paul S. Boyer, ed., *The Oxford Companion to United States History* (New York, 2001), 666-69.

[17] John L. Bullion, "Stamp Act" in Boyer, *Oxford Companion*, 741-42 and Troy Kickler, "Stamp Act" *NorthCarolinahistory.org: An Online Encyclopedia*, North Carolina History Project, www.northcarolinahis-

tory.org/encyclopedia/237/entry
(accessed July 1, 2013).

[18] Troy Kickler, "Sons of Liberty" *NorthCarolinahistory.org: An Online Encyclopedia*, North Carolina History Project, http://www.northcarolinahistory.org/encyclopedia/240/entry (accessed July 1, 2013; Buillon, "Stamp Act," *Oxford Companion*, 732; Murray N. Rothbard, *Conceived in Liberty Vol. III* (Auburn, Alabama: reprint, 1999); Robert L. Ganyard, *Emergence*, 17-18; Powell, *North Carolina*, 163.

[19] Bullion, "Stamp Act," *The Oxford Companion*, 742.

[20] McConville, "Revolutionary War," *The Oxford Companion*, 666-67.

[21] Powell, *North Carolina*, 139.

[22] Griffith I. McRee, *Life and Correspondence of James Iredell, One of The Associate Justices of the Supreme Court of The United States, Vol. I* (New York, reprint, 1949), 275.

[23] Dan Higginbotham, *The Papers of James Iredell, Vol. I, 1767-1777* (Raleigh, 1976), 187.

[24] Higginbotham, *Papers of James Iredell*, 175, 211.

[25] Ibid, 196; Lindley S. Butler and Alan D. Watson, eds., *The North Carolina Experience: An Interpretive & Documentary History* (Chapel Hill, 1984), 138; McRee, *Life and Correspondence of James Iredell*, 1: 274.

[26] "Postal Rider," May 6, 1775. Cupola House Association, Edenton, North Carolina. In 1788, two newspapers were based in Edenton—*Intelligencer* and *State Gazette*. The latter had been originally located in New Bern.

[27] McRee, *Life and Correspondence of James Iredell*, 1: 268-70; John Paul Jones to Joseph Hewes, May 19, 1776, North Illinois Library, http://lincoln.lib.niu.edu/cgi-bin/amarch/getdoc.pl?/var/lib/philologic/databases/amarch/.16303
(accessed July 1, 2013).

[28] Troy L. Kickler, "Edenton Tea Party: An American First." *Carolina Journal.* March 2006.

[29] Ibid.; "Association Signed by Ladies of Edenton, North Carolina, 25 October 1774," in Don Higginbotham, " Decision for Revolution" in Lindley S. Butler & Alan D. Watson, eds., *The North Carolina Experience: An Interpretive & Documentary History* (Chapel Hill, 1984), 136-37.

[30] Kickler, "Edenton Tea Party: An American First," *NorthCarolinahistory.org: An Online Encyclopedia*, North Carolina History Project, http://northcarolinahistory.org/commentary/20 (accessed July 1, 2013).

[31] Kickler, "Edenton Tea Party," *Carolina Journal*, March 2006 and Powell, *North Carolina, 169-71.* For more on what is now called the Edenton Tea Party, please see Richard Dillard, "Historic Tea Party of Edenton" in *The North Carolina Booklet*, vol. 23 (Raleigh, 1926); Linda K. Kerber, *Women of the Republic: Intellect and Ideology in Revolutionary America* (Chapel Hill, 1980); Lou Rogers Wehlitz, *Tar Heel Women* (Raleigh, 1949).

[32] Higginbotham, ed., *Papers of James Iredell*, 1: 340-41.

[33] Ibid.

[34] Ibid; Ganyard, *Emergence*, 47-48.

[35] Ganyard, *Emergence*, 47.

[36] "Resolutions by inhabitants of Chowan County concerning resistance to Parliamentary taxation and the Provincial Congress of North Carolina," in *Colonial and State Records of North Carolina, Vol. 9*, 1037-38.

[37] Ibid.

[38] Kellie Slappey, "The Test," *NorthCarolinahistory.org: An Online Encyclopedia*, North Carolina History Project, http://northcaroli-

nahistory.org/encyclopedia/464/entry
(accessed July 1, 2013) and Kellie Slappey, "Rev. Daniel Earl."
NorthCarolinahistory.org: An Online Encyclopedia, North Carolina
History Project, http://northcarolinahistory.org/encyclopedia/467/
entry
(accessed July 1, 2013).

[39] Donna Kelly and Lang Baradell, eds., *The Papers of James Iredell,
Vol. III, 1784-1789,*
68.

[40] James Iredell, Sr., "To The Inhabitants of Great Britain" in
McRee, ed., *Life and Correspondence of James Iredell,* 1: 205-20.

[41] Ibid.

[42] Thomas Jefferson, *Summary View of the Rights of British America* in
The Avalon Project: Documents in Law, History and Diplomacy. Located at http://avalon.law.yale.edu/18th_century/jeffsumm.asp
(accessed July, 2013).

[43] James Iredell, Sr., "Principles of an American Whig" in McRee,
ed., *Life and Correspondence of James* Iredell, 1: 245-54.

[44] Ibid.

[45] Ibid.

[46] Ibid.

[47] McRee, *Life and Correspondence of James Iredell,* 196-97.

[48] Higginbotham, *Papers of James Iredell,* 1: 414.

[49] Troy Kickler, "Joseph Hewes." *NorthCarolinahistory.org.* For
more on Hewes, please see William Brown and Charles Peters,
Biography of the Signers to the Declaration of Independence.
John Sanders and Robert Waln, eds. Vol. 5. (Philadelphia Press,
1828); John Frost, *Lives of American Merchants: Eminent for
Integrity, Enterprise, and Public Spirit.* (Saxton and Miles,
1846); Robert W. Lincoln, *Lives of the Presidents of the United*

States: With Biographical Notices of the Signers of the Declaration of Independence. (Published by Edward Kearny, 1842); Willis P. Whichard, *Justice James Iredell.* (Carolina Academic Press, 2000).

[50] Higginbotham, "Decision for Revolution," in Butler and Watson, eds., *North Carolina Experience*, 134, and Powell, *North Carolina*, 184.

[51] John W. Moore, *School History of North Carolina, From 1584 to the Present Time* (New York, 1882), 115-16; Ganyard, 69; Higginbotham, *Papers of James Iredell,* I:339-41.

[52] Ganyard, *Emergence*, 71, 80-81.

[53] Ganyard, *Emergence*, 72-81. William S. Powell, "Thomas Jones" in Powell, ed., *Dictionary of North Carolina Biography*, Vol. 3: 328.

[54] Moore, *History of North Carolina*, 115-16.

[55] Ganyard, *Emergence*, 77; Powell, *North Carolina*, 186.

[56] Ganyard, *Emergence,* 80-82.

[57] *Ibid.,* 85-86.

[58] Ibid;, Powell, *North Carolina*, 172; Moore, *History of North Carolina*, 116.

[59] Powell, *North Carolina*, 218.

[60] Powell, *North Carolina*, 185-86; Ganyard, *Emergence*, 69.

[61] Jeff Broadwater, "Bayard v. Singleton" *NorthCarolinahistory.org: An Online Encyclopedia*, North Carolina History Project, http://northcarolinahistory.org/encyclopedia/117/entry (accessed July 1, 2013).

[62] Ibid.; Whichard, *Iredell*, 9-16.

[63] Broadwater, "Bayard v. Singleton," NorthCarolinahistory.org; Moore, *History of North Carolina*, 116.

64 J. Edwin Hendricks, " Joining the Federal Union" in Butler and Watson, eds., *The North Carolina Experience*, 150; Willis Whichard, *Justice James Iredell* (Durham, 2000), 9-16.

65 Whichard, *Iredell*, 9-16.

66 Broadwater, "Bayard v. Singleton."

67 Daniel Dreisbach, "Founders Famous and Forgotten," *The Intercollegiate Review* Vol. 42, No.2: 3-12.

68 Troy Kickler, "Hugh Williamson" *NorthCarolinahistory.org: An Online Encyclopedia*, North Carolina History Project, http:// northcarolinahistory.org/encyclopedia/275/entry (accessed July 1, 2013); and Kickler, "Recognizing a Forgotten Founder," *The Imaginative Conservative*, April 30, 2011. Located at www.theimaginativeconservative.org (accessed July1, 2013). For more on Williamson, please see Bruce R. Dain, *A Hideous Monster of the Mind: American Race Theory in the Early Republic* (Cambridge, Massachusetts, 2003); John L. Humber, "Hugh Williamson," in *Dictionary of North Carolina Biography*, ed. William S. Powell (Chapel Hill, 1996); John R. Vile, *The Constitutional Convention of 1787: A Comprehensive Encyclopedia of America's Founding* (Santa Barbara, 2005); Hugh Williamson, *The History of North Carolina* (Philadelphia, 1812).

69 Powell, *North Carolina*, 223-25.

70 Ibid.

71 Kelly and Bardell, eds., *Papers of James Iredell*, 3: xxxix.

72 Whichard, *Iredell*, 44-45.

73 Troy Kickler, "Forward" in Kyle Scott, *The Federalist Papers* (New York, 2012), xii.

74 Powell, *North Carolina*, 225-29.

75 Kelly and Bardell, eds., *Papers of James Iredell*, 3: 371-73. The eighty-five essays were written to persuade primarily New Yorkers

to ratify the Constitution; however, Hamilton, Madison, and Jay knew others elsewhere would be readers.

[76] Colleen A. Sheehan, and Gary L. McDowell, eds. *Friends of the Constitution: Writings of the "Other" Federalists, 1787-1788* (Indianapolis, 1998).

[77] Ibid.

[78] Kickler, "Recognizing a Forgotten Founder."

[79] Ibid., Hugh Williamson, "Remarks on a New Plan of Government" in Sheehan and McDowell, eds., *Friends of the Constitution.*

[80] Jeff Broadwater, *George Mason: Forgotten Founder* (Chapel Hill, 2006), 210-11; Willis P. Whichard, "James Iredell, Sr." *NorthCarolinahistory.org: An Online Encyclopedia*, North Carolina History Project, http://northcarolinahistory.org/encyclopedia/105/entry (accessed July 1, 2013).

[81] George Mason, "Objections to This Constitution of Government." Located at www.constitution.org/gmason/objections.html (accessed July 1, 2013).

[82] Marcus, "Answers to Mr. Mason's Objections to the New Constitution recommended by the late Convention at Philadelphia" in Kelly and Bardell, eds., *Papers of James Iredell*, III: 341; Kermit L. Hall and Mark David Hall, eds., *The Collected Works of James Wilson* (Indianapolis, 2007) Vol. I, xxii. Entire Iredell manuscript can be in found Kelly and Bardell, 3: 341-70.

[83] Kelly and Bardell, eds., *Papers of James Iredell* Vol 3: 371-73.

[84] Whichard, "Iredell," NorthCarolinahistory.org.

[85] *Proceedings and Debates of the Convention of North-Carolina, Convened at Hillsborough, on Monday the 21st Day of July, 1788, for the Purpose of Deliberating and Determining on the Constitution Recommended by the General Convention at Philadelphia, the 17th Day of September, 1787: To Which is Prefixed the Said Constitution.* This primary source can be located online at http://

docsouth.unc.edu/nc/conv1788/menu.html.

[86] Pauline Maeir, *Ratification: The People Debate the Constitution* (New York, 2010), 411.

[87] David Koon, "Hillsborough Convention of 1788," *NorthCarolinahistory.org: An Online Encyclopedia*, North Carolina History Project, http://northcarolinahistory.org/encyclopedia/276/entry (accessed July 1, 2013).

[88] Maeir, Ratification, 403-23.

[89] Ibid.; Kelly and Bardell, eds., *Papers of James Iredell*, 3: 413.

[90] Hendricks, "Joining the Federal Union" in Butler and Watson, ed., *North Carolina Experience*, 155.

[91] Hugh Williamson, "Apology" in Butler and Watson, eds., *The North Carolina Experience*, 165-67.

[92] Hendricks, "Joining the Federal Union," 155-56.

[93] "Exchange of Addresses between the Independent State of North Carolina and the Newly Elected President of the United States" in Butler and Watson, eds., *The North Carolina Experience*, 167-68.

[94] Whichard, *Iredell*, 266.

[95] Kermit L. Hall and Mark David Hall, eds., *Collected Works of James Wilson, Volume I* (Indianapolis, 2007), xvi.

[96] Ibid., xi, 401.

[97] Ibid., xix-xxv.

[98] Ibid.

[99] Ibid; Whichard, *Iredell*, 267.

[100] Hall and Hall, eds., *Collected Works of James Wilson*, Vol. 1: xxv-xxvi; Whichard, *Iredell*, 269.

[101] Whichard, *Iredell*, 110.

[102] Ibid., 102-103.

[103] Ibid., 97-109.

[104] Ibid., 131-35. Iredell helped start a centuries-old American legal debate. In *Calder v. Bull*, Chase argued that the Court could overturn an act of a legislature, in this case a state legislature, if the act violated the social compact. That action would be an unjust law; in fact, according to Chase, a legislative act that violates natural law theory is not even a law. Iredell disagreed. His argument was basically that the framers had defined legislative power and that an action that violated its constitution may be considered void. But Iredell doubted that a court could declare it void because it deemed a legislative act to violate something outside the Constitution—natural law. In short, an Edentonian helped shape Americans current understanding of the *ex post facto* clause and contributed to an over two-centuries-old debate, involving such notables as Supreme Court Justice Hugo Black and Justice John Paul Stevens, regarding whether natural law can be invoked to overturn a legislative act.

[105] Ibid., 166-71.

[106] Ibid., 100.

[107] Ibid., 287-88.

[108] Ibid., 289; Bernard Bailyn, *The Ideological Origins of the American Revolution* (Cambridge, MS, 1967), 328.

CPSIA information can be obtained at www.ICGtesting.com
Printed in the USA
BVOW02s0306121213

338912BV00001B/2/P